D0282978

Time and Tide in Acadia

ALSO BY CHRISTOPHER CAMUTO

A Fly Fisherman's Blue Ridge (1990)

⑤

Another Country (1997)

⑤

Hunting from Home (2003)

Time and Tide in Acadia

SEASONS ON MOUNT DESERT ISLAND

Christopher Camuto

THE COUNTRYMAN PRESS

WOODSTOCK, VERMONT

LIBRARY
FRANKLIN PIERCE UNIVERSITY
RINDGE NH 03461

Copyright © 2009, 2010 by Christopher Camuto

All rights reserved

Printed in the United States of America
Originally published in hardcover in 2009 by W. W. Norton & Company, Inc.
First Paperback Edition published in 2010 by The Countryman Press

"Expressions of Sea Level," copyright © 1964 by A. R. Ammons, from
The Selected Poems, expanded edition, by A. R. Ammons.
Used by permission of W. W. Norton & Company, Inc.

Photographs by Christopher Camuto

For information about permission to reproduce selections from this book,
write to Permissions, W. W. Norton & Company, Inc.,
500 Fifth Avenue, New York, NY 10110

For information about special discounts for bulk purchases, please contact
W. W. Norton Special Sales at specialsales@wwnorton.com or 800-233-4830

Manufacturing by Versa Press
Book design by Ellen Cipriano

Library of Congress Cataloging-in-Publication Data

Camuto, Christopher.
Time and tide in Acadia : seasons on Mount Desert Island / Christopher
Camuto. — 1st ed.
p. cm.
Includes bibliographical references.
ISBN 978-0-393-06067-6 (hardcover)
ISBN 978-0-88150-912-0 (paperback)
1. Natural history—Maine—Mount Desert Island. 2. Natural history—Maine—
Acadia National Park. 3. Natural areas—Maine—Mount Desert Island.
4. Natural areas—Maine—Acadia National Park. 5. Mount Desert Island (Me.)
6. Acadia National Park (Me.) I. Title.
QH105.M2C36 2009 2010
508.741'45—dc22

2009001693

Published by
The Countryman Press
P.O. Box 748, Woodstock, VT 05091
www.countrymanpress.com

Distributed by
W. W. Norton & Company, Inc.
500 Fifth Avenue, New York, NY 10110
www.wwnorton.com

1 2 3 4 5 6 7 8 9 0

For my sisters
—Mary, Pat, and Kathi—
and the Maine of childhood

The same day we passed also near to an island about four or five leagues long, in the neighborhood of which we just escaped being lost on a little rock on a level with the water, which made an opening in our barque near the keel. From this island to the main land on the north, the distance is less than a hundred paces. It is very high, and notched in places, so that there is the appearance to one at sea, as of seven or eight mountains extending along near each other. The summit of the most of them is destitute of trees, as there are only rocks on them. The woods consist of pines, firs, and birches only. I named it Isle des Monts Déserts. The latitude is 44° 30'.

—SAMUEL DE CHAMPLAIN,
SEPTEMBER 5, 1604

Contents

CONTENTS

ACKNOWLEDGMENTS

I am grateful to Jennifer Lyons, my patient agent, and to Amy Cherry, my equally patient editor, for their interest in this project. Bucknell University granted me leave time and travel assistance for part of this work, and the College of the Atlantic in Bar Harbor gave permission and logistical support for my visit to Mount Desert Rock in October of 2006. Chuck Whitney and Toby Stephenson did yeoman work organizing that trip. Thanks to the Abbe Museum in Bar Harbor, for providing access to Mount Desert's indigenous past, and to the Friends of Acadia, which puts so much volunteer effort into maintaining the trails of Acadia National Park. Thanks to the Maine Audubon Society, for the genius of its autumn pelagic-bird cruise, and to the naturalists of Allied Whale, who do such a fine job of educating the public about the marine life of the Gulf of Maine on whale-watch cruises out of Bar Harbor. At Bucknell University, graduate assistants Kimi Cunningham Grant and Cara Maria Cambardella helped with research, photo-editing, and proofreading. Erica Stern kept the proceedings in order from New York; from her vantage in Maine, Kathleen Brandes put her keen weather eye on the text as copy editor. Mary Jellison found me a comfortable, warbler-infested place to stay on the "Quietside" of Mount Desert Island and introduced me to a wonderful circle of friends. Special thanks to Andy Ciotola and Katie Hays for coming down from Damariscotta for a good walk at Ship Harbor, where this book begins. Finally, gratitude is due the National Park Service, which works every day to preserve the heart and soul of Mount Desert Island, giving us all a chance to visit what is left of *l'Acadie*.

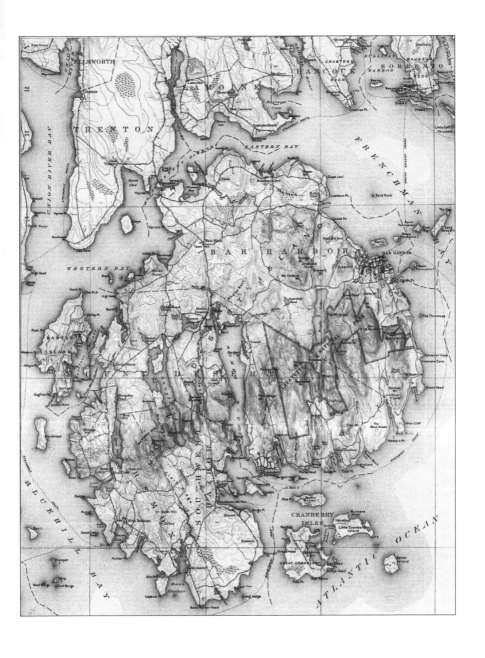

Time and Tide in Acadia

·   ·   ·   ·   ·   ·   ·

*L*and lies in water . . .

—ELIZABETH BISHOP,
"THE MAP"

FIRST LIGHT—

Land's End and the Mind's Eye

Sunrise from Cadillac Mountain reveals a coastline carved with a crooked knife.

From that famous vantage on Mount Desert Island, the coast of Maine comes out of the dark as a complicated affair of peninsulas and coves, a jigsaw of rock and water, a play of motion and stasis. The ground you stand on—granite—is as firm as bedrock gets, but the other elements—air, water, light—move fluidly through a landscape that seems simultaneously ancient and just born. The mainland is an afterthought, something to put an edge on.

At dawn, the familiar names of famous places don't much matter—Bar Harbor, Frenchman Bay, the Porcupine Islands, the Cranberry Isles. You need pay attention only to the forms of this landscape emerging from night, a natural reciprocity of land and water shaped by climate and honed by weather, attended by the casual genius of sea level expressing itself as a restless edge of tide.

On Cadillac you can feel all of Mount Desert underfoot. You seem to be riding a graceful surfacing of mountains headed, like a pod of whales, out to sea through other, smaller islands equally well wrought, unique expressions of rock foaming at their margins, leaning a little seaward or a little landward, depending on which way the tide is moving. From here, to the south and west, one island leads to another, all the way to Frenchboro and Swans Island and Isle au Haut, as this landscape toys with the idea of islands until the sea says *enough* and there is only water.

On clear mornings, standing on this great whaleback of granite, with this wide coastal world at your feet, you can see the roundness of the earth in your mind's eye and sense keenly the orderliness of the solar system, the way the sun and the moon pull on the oceans to the advantage of life on earth. To the east beyond Schoodic and Petit Manan, you can see a day coming toward you as a blush of light—the "rosy-fingered dawn" of Homeric poetry.

Dawn on Cadillac is frequently greeted by small crowds—larger ones on the solstices and equinoxes—that gather on this well-worn summit, though natives and seasoned visitors have their own, more private places from which to watch the rising sun. I don't like crowds either, but come once, at least, to Cadillac Mountain to see the sun rise Down East. Watch the ragged beauty of this well-built coast—an affair of granite and spruce-fir—casually reappear out of night.

On a cool morning in autumn, you will find clusters of people wrapped around cups of coffee and hot chocolate, and couples, wrapped around each other, drawn to the ordinary business of the turning earth—a sleepy, makeshift tribe wanting to see the sun come up in a beautiful place. Some cheer and clap at the performance—partly as a joke, I think, and partly to relieve their embarrassment at being unexpectedly moved and suddenly more innocent than they could imagine themselves being.

Watch enough dawns from enough places on Mount Desert, in every season and in all weather, and eventually you might get a glimpse of *Pemetic*,* the Mount Desert of the Passamaquoddy, wielders of the crooked knife, who gathered food and hunted and fashioned their creation myths and stories on these shores. The Passamaquoddy are Abenaki—"those living at the sunrise"—Algonquin-speaking people who, along with the Penobscot, Maliseet, Pennacook, and Micmac, understood well the nature of this place.

Mount Desert Island has long been famous as the largest and most mountainous of Maine's coastal islands, a roughly ten-mile-by-ten-mile wolf's paw of granite between Blue Hill Bay and Frenchman Bay. Mount Desert is also famous for Acadia National Park, which preserves two-thirds of the island as relatively undeveloped, and for the seasonally bustling town of Bar Harbor, which embraced its fate as a popular tourist destination a century and a half ago.

---

* Literally, "a range of mountains." Fannie Hardy Eckstrom, "Indian Place-Names of the Penobscot Valley and Maine Coast," *The Maine Bulletin* 44, no. 4 (November 1941).

Mount Desert has a long, well-documented history of being discovered and rediscovered, a history exhaustively written about elsewhere. The island was within the territory of the Abenaki at the time of European exploration. The French explorer Samuel de Champlain gave Mount Desert its current name in 1604, discovering it for the French at the same time the English were making their claims on what was to become the coast of Maine. During the seventeenth and eighteenth centuries, fishermen, farmers, quarrymen, and other working people discovered Mount Desert as a place to live and labor. They learned to use the island and the Gulf of Maine as well in their way as the Abenaki had, and accommodated themselves to its weather, seasons, and resources.

When Mount Desert was discovered by artists in the nineteenth century, it became a source of images—realistic and Romantic—that took their place in American landscape painting. The island's landforms, seascapes, colors, light, and weather were and remain irresistible to painters and photographers. In the work of Thomas Cole and Frederic Church, among others, Mount Desert entered high culture and, eventually, popular American consciousness. The beauty that drew artists soon drew a steady stream of tourists and, eventually, wealthy summer residents to the island. After the Civil War, especially, Mount Desert became a favorite place for hikers who created the need for and helped build the island's wonderful trails, detailed maps of which began to appear in the late 1860s, along with field guides to the island's backcountry. In the 1930s, the Civilian Conservation Corps did extensive work on Acadia National Park's trails and roads.

It is difficult to account with words for the appeal of the coast of Maine. Land's end is one thing and many things on Mount

Desert Island: coves and headlands, bold stretches of rock cliff and intricate salt marshes, foaming ledges and still deepwater anchorages, blue glacial lakes where landlocked salmon hide and reedy green ponds where mergansers raise flotillas of young, glacial valleys carpeted with meadows fit for deer and moose, cliffs where peregrine falcons nest, wooded streams where ovenbirds and winter wrens mouse around mossy stumps and fallen timber alongside pools where brook trout rise.

Everywhere on Mount Desert, life is compressed between great forces—terrestrial and marine—that have carved out innumerable ecological niches. Life thrives with heartening diversity. And the larger look of the landscape—the rugged, inviting sweep of it—has a psychological appeal that never wears out. The Mongolians have a saying about the Gobi—that sometimes you have to go down to the desert to stretch your soul. Mount Desert Island is like that, a soul-stretching place. Millions visit at least once; some of us never stop coming back.

After a decade of work in the cove forests of the southern Appalachians—being tutored by rivers and mountains and old-growth forest—I was drawn to the coast of Maine seven or eight years ago and to Mount Desert Island in particular. The appeal of this famous landscape needs no argument or explanation. I had been to Mount Desert and Acadia once as a child but harbor only the dimmest memories of that visit. A family reunion, prompted by my sisters, brought me back. After great days hiking the mountains with nieces and nephews, who were on the verge of molting into adulthood, I realized I had found another landscape to spend time in as a writer, a place to stretch my legs and thoughts, to observe and learn and, eventually, to account for in writing the time I have spent here.

Like others who come to love Mount Desert Island, I learned that there was an art to discovering it on the personal level, and I eventually found ways to get away from the crowds. I tried to slip past the island's picturesque appeal into a more elemental experience of it. Preferring observation to recreation, I strove to get beyond a framed landscape to an unframed experience of the nature of this coast. I pursued what I call in my journals *field moments*—unexpected encounters with the life or look of things, the traditional anchors of a nature writer's awareness of place and of self in place. I found this landscapes quietly compelling in ways I try to convey in the pages that follow, which I offer as a companion, not a guide, to anyone else's walking and paddling here—a conversation with others who enjoy Mount Desert's profound appeal. As a writer, I imagine the reader not as someone who needs entertaining but as someone who might want to take a slow walk on a good trail or paddle a canoe in quiet water.

Eventually I found a modest cabin to rent—mostly in spring, early summer, and then again in fall—on a quiet recess of an anchorage on the western side of the island, not quite on the water but within sight of it through a screen of birch and spruce thick with singing warblers and kibitzing crows. One glorious year, I contrived to get to Mount Desert before the hardwoods leafed out and did not leave until they were bare. Even then, I left wanting to stay until king eiders and red-throated loons appeared offshore and snowstorms filled the spruce with cold, quiet hours.

In central Pennsylvania, where I struggle with a shabby, eighty-acre woodland farm, I have to put up with a Sunday rush hour of buggy traffic as my Amish neighbors make their way to church. On Mount Desert, rush hour was an affair of lobster boats. At my cabin I had the luxury of two wake-up calls—the throbbing of a neighbor's diesel idling to life at 4:15 a.m. and another—a slacker, I guess—grumbling in the fog at 5. Especially given the early daylight Down East, 4 or 5 a.m. is a decent hour for a writer to wrap himself around a cup of coffee, or for a hiker or paddler to get his gear together. Sometimes during breakfast I'd listen to the marine channel on the radio as the boats went out, and I'd laugh at the laconic chatter and rude jokes.

For the most part, I did what anyone does when they keep coming back to Mount Desert Island. I hiked Acadia's quiet trails, explored its marshes, ponds, and lakes in a canoe, and paddled its marine edges in a kayak. I sought out the island within the island and tried to educate myself about what I was seeing. My time on the island was more social than these solitary essays convey. Especially out of season, Mount Desert is a friendly place, congenial for talking about jazz, politics, and travel as well as nature. But I'm not interested in conveying anecdotes here. I merely try to bring the reader to the edges of places and moments—summits, tidal pools, marshes—where some experience revealed an aspect of Mount Desert's inner life.

Mount Desert Island and Acadia National Park are endlessly suggestive, endlessly rewarding. Mount Desert is all vantage—not just its famous summits but its unnamed places as well. Every turn of trail opens some new space in its interior, every reach of water opens another threshold in the horizon, every step or paddle stroke improves depth of field. No day is ever the same, no season. You especially learn to enjoy the way every hour here is quickened by the rise and fall of the tide. Time slowly hurries here in ways it *takes* time getting used to, eddies into still moments, and then moves on. Once you give in to the offbeat rhythm of the tide, the island enlarges with good hours and you realize that you will never get to the bottom of it and never stop coming back.

What follows are attempts to capture hours and especially field moments that arose all over Mount Desert Island, often in Acadia National Park, attempts to assay the underlying poetics of this landscape—the relation of words and things—to understand the appeal of its deep ecology, to see what nature reveals to the curiosity of someone drawn, as many of us are, to the edge of sea. The genius of Mount Desert reveals itself in unexpected experiences so vivid they might seem imagined, moments that will leave you feeling simultaneously at home and profoundly estranged—the essence of the experience of the *uncanny*—the sudden, shook-silk rustling of an eider's wings in the fog on a cold spring morning, the gleaming antlers of a whitetail deer rising out of the spartina of a salt marsh on an autumn evening, the cry of young peregrine falcons in the rain, or a noon-silent white-throated sparrow perched in a pitch pine twisting out of a fissure in granite, reaching toward the sun.

WOLFTREE FARM
Millmont, Pennsylvania
June 2008

The tides are in our veins.

—ROBINSON JEFFERS,
"CONTINENT'S END"

AT SHIP HARBOR—

The Edge of the Sea

Time and *tide* are cognate, words with a common root.

You can see that in the rocky throat of Ship Harbor any morning, hear it in the insistent rush of water to which the lives of eiders, gulls, and osprey, among much else, are finely tuned.

Dawn reveals a murmuring riffle of tidal flow out of a narrow opening in the coast between Bennet Cove and Bass Harbor Head, opposite Great Gott Island. Approaching low tide, the water in Ship Harbor slides seaward like a river over a cobble bar perhaps a hundred yards long and half as wide toward a quiet bay mouth between two unnamed headlands. As the shallow embayment drains, the Gulf of Maine waits, a shimmering gray weave bulging with new hours.

Come here some foggy morning at low tide in late May and

you will feel time keenly. Breathe salt air full of the scent of balsam fir and spruce and tidal funk. Listen to the offbeat, nasal burr of black-throated green warblers and the quick, rising *ʒiiiiiip* of northern parulas hidden in those dark conifers. Perhaps the long, well-modulated call of a white-throated sparrow or the fluting of a hermit thrush comes through the woods to your ears.

A fading sea breeze rustles the stiff-branched heaths at the woods' edge, a tangle of leathery-leaved shrubs where a ragged-looking snowshoe hare nervously bides its time waiting to make a foray into the rockweed. Here at the channel, an ebbing tide sifts itself through time-worn stones. Slender herring gulls slice through the gray air between those granite headlands beyond which everything else is lost to view in fog.

In the foreground, slabs of pink granite whitened by the sun have calved off two weathered brows of spruce-darkened land and slid in a jumble toward a narrow tidal passage blackened with rockweed. Over thousands of winters, the massive sheets of rock in this quarry have slowly burst at their seams into jagged chunks that lean a little seaward until they fall or are gathered by storms into the tidal zone. There they are worn so round that they wobble in the tide, pivoting like boiling eggs until they become perfectly sculpted cobbles. Over time, these cobbles are worn down and become small stones that roll in the soft wash of low tide, clicking faintly, glistening like treasure.

The monumental granite of the tidal zone looks like a great worked edge a long time in the making, which, of course, it is— flakes, blanks, and *débitage* from some great tool fashioning, some incessant concussive labor at the sea's edge.

On the coast of Maine, deep time casually insists on itself at every point—in the curl of moon-turned ocean at land's end, in the soft rattle of these colorful wet stones, in the clutch of spruce roots on algae-blackened granite, and in the birdlife that learned, thousands of generations ago, to winter or to nest or to feed here during migration.

In mid-May, when I typically arrive on the island, wintering birds are long gone and nesting has begun for other species. Warblers seem to appear with every gust of wind. The understory hardwoods are just leafing in, the blooms of cherry and shadbush adding color to the dark, spruce-fir woods through which I've walked to get to the Ship Harbor channel. Red squirrels noisily defend territory nothing contests. Small flocks of crows occasionally echo their agitation. The shattered forms of this winter's cull of dead spruce, fir, and birch lay scattered about, a splintered crop of new nursery logs that will host a century of moss, lichens, fungi, and insect life.

If I could come to only one place on Mount Desert Island, it would be here, to the quiet environs around Ship Harbor, an oddly named body of water given its shallow depth and modest reach. There are no ships in the tidal pond that spreads inland from this rock-lined channel.* At low tide, this water barely floats the gulls and cormorants that come to feed on crabs and sculpins and the other marine life that takes its chances here. I frequently come to the channel in the throat of Ship Harbor because this is

---

* The distinguished historian Samuel Eliot Morison explains that the name derived from an incident in the War of Independence during which a local vessel escaped from an English man-of-war by running the channel at high water, only to find itself grounded fast at low tide. See *The Story of Mount Desert Island*, page 103.

where, to my eye, the tide runs keenest—seconds and minutes of seawater straining through an hourglass of granite.

Here, at the Ship Harbor channel, I can stand at the wrack line at ebb tide on a cool spring morning poised between the forest and the sea, the primal situation in Abenaki mythology: "In the beginning there was only the forest and the sea. . . ." And, standing here, you think, yes, that would be enough to set everything in motion.

All creation myths serve to remind us that human life walked onto a stage already established, that human consciousness awoke in nature as it was, its forces and processes already in play. Standing here on a cool, foggy May morning, poised between rock gripped by the roots of white spruce and rock gripped by the quiet white reach of a tide about to turn, I feel as human beings have always felt when face to face with nature— "the circumstance which dwarfs every other circumstance," to use Emerson's fine phrase—both large and small, a part of things and other. The seacoast is, quite literally, uncanny— home and not home.

Laughing gulls cry rudely over the exposed tidal zone embracing the abandonment of the rockweeds, barnacles, kelp, and sea mosses that have to wait out hours of desiccation, the desolate and unsettling landscape exposed to view by low tide. Despite the haunting beauty of these hours, and the way the stalling tidal set draws on all your senses, enlivening your awareness of place, in the echo of those raucous cries you feel gulled by time, left behind, eddied out of currents as difficult to follow with the mind as with the eye, not as much a part of things as you planned to be when you slung a worn, canvas day pack, half filled with books and food, over your shoulder at the trailhead on your way to find your niche in the deep ecology of this coast.

I'm sitting in the shadow of some white spruce and balsam fir on a comfortable shelf of bedrock just above the spring-tide wrack line. I can hear the trill of a yellow-rumped warbler in the foggy woods on the opposite side of the channel. As the thinning fog sifts through the evergreens, I let my attention shift from the quiet harbor to the bay mouth and the two worn headlands that face the Gulf of Maine. The Bass Harbor foghorn sounds its warning. Gulls materialize and disappear. Mallards hustle inland. The quiet rush of the tide in the channel underwrites the occasional, rattling call of that yellow-rump, which on account of the fog seems closer than it is.

I draw a water bottle out of my canvas pack, along with some bread, cheese, and fruit—neither breakfast nor lunch—and settle myself next to a small cairn of possessions—the notebook, field guides, binoculars of an organized intruder intent on taking things in as best he can, the gear not of studying but of learning as nothing more, or less, than observation. What else is there to do here—or anywhere in nature—but to indulge the awareness of your senses, observe the instructive otherness that lies just beyond—or is it *within*—the beauty of nature, and improve your understanding of the world around you and of yourself as an observing being?

An osprey flies up over the conifers that line the opposite headland in thick ranks, the long, bent-wing shape of the bird unmistakable as it stalls over one of the tallest trees, its shaggily feathered legs well clawed with open talons that give it a right of purchase anywhere. Like bald eagles, osprey are a common but striking sight here, and with their craggy-skulled, fierce-eyed presence, one of the great warrior shapes of nature, predatory to a fault—not *common* at all—painted starkly in black and white, a hovering hunter that must freeze the heart it dives on.

The osprey settles into a spruce, folding itself within dark green boughs, suddenly becoming—as if I were witness to a myth—the great tree's keen eyes. Even though I know it's there, once the tree accommodates itself to the folded bird, the osprey is hard to find.

I eat, watching the channel, the woods, the still harbor to one side of me and what I can see of the gray, ruffled gulf to the other—both still lightly wreathed in a fog that will burn off by midmorning. Now and then I look for the osprey hidden in that dark symmetry of spruce. The bird is eventually betrayed by its white feathers, around which the mind's eye reorganizes the shape of its shadowed form, its bulk impressive even from a distance.

I accept the osprey in the spruce as one thing now, as the keen eyes of the coast this morning, life well joined as raptor and conifer—and well situated to be what it is in this guise, the quick consciousness of one being joined with the still consciousness of another. And this, I think, is what the edge of the sea tends to do, juxtapose what is fixed and fluid in nature to the advantage of both.

I have come here many times over the years to watch the tide turn in the Ship Harbor channel, sometimes intending to sit and observe the exact moment when the outflow over the bar finally ceases and the standing wave behind which eiders feed becomes the leading edge of the next flood tide.

The clear riffle over the bar is braided like the rushing shallows of a mountain trout stream. If you had the patience and resisted all the distractions of this place, you ought to be able to see the precise moment when that tidal stream stalled and the broad wave-form waiting in the deeper water beyond the bar leaned into the channel as the tide changed.

But I have learned what anyone would, that watching the tide turn is a fool's venture, a dogged exercise in a self-absorbed goal and, like watching the clock, not a good way to use the hours. In the end, you will be distracted by the life of things here—the face of a harbor seal, the silhouette of a bald eagle, the diligence of a lobster boat, or the imperious tack of a yacht—and the tide will be flowing back into Ship Harbor without your having seen the casually momentous change. The tide turns well enough unwatched and, rising or falling, it marks the hours here with a steady, impartial hand.

The point of coming to the edge of the sea is to give yourself over to those hours, to the familiar otherness of what Rachel Carson called the "elusive and indefinable boundary" between the marine and the terrestrial realms—a dynamic environment that stirred the evolution of life on earth and continues to challenge science to explain its life forms and ecosystems. The edge of the sea naturally attracts our curiosity, stimulates our imaginations—it was artists, after all, who first drew popular attention to Mount Desert Island—and stirs our spirits with an enlarged sense of what life is.

A greater black-backed gull perches on a rock in the channel seaward of where I sit this morning to watch the outflow from Ship Harbor build into that standing wave in the bay mouth. The black-back brays mulishly, calling its mate or asserting some territorial claim none of the smaller species of gulls dare challenge. Unless the osprey chooses to assert its prerogatives, or a bald eagle wheels overhead, the large, aggressive black-back holds sway over the fishing to be done this morning in the nourishing waters on the sea side of the channel.

The cry of this most magisterial of gulls is raw and full throated, and when the bird is at full gape, you can see its whole body quivering with the aggressive force of a self-assertion that nearly lifts it off its granite perch. Only immature herring gulls, mottled with inexperience, come near it. But they retreat quickly when the large bird unfolds its broad wings and stomps its scaly legs in agitation.

A commanding bird in flight—hinting at characteristics of hawk, osprey, and eagle in those powerful wings—the well-named greater black-back nearly bursts the evolutionary seams of what a gull is. If the herring gull, so graceful a part of coastal life, is the platonic form of the family of gulls—the Laridae—the greater black-back is clearly an exaggeration of what all other gulls are, a beautifully extreme case, so strongly wrought it seems halfway something other than a gull. In any event, this black-back and its mate now glean the channel for mussels and crabs, governing what all the other gulls do here this morning.

Fog drifts thinly through the ranks of spruce across the way. In the still water of the harbor side of the channel bar, a great blue heron wades the quiet shore, poised in its hair-trigger way. An assembly of angled legs, curved neck, and dagger beak, the slender bird seems out of place at this rough tidal edge. Thirty yards away, the heron hasn't seen me yet and hunts—for its fishing looks more like hunting—slowly toward me.

Unlike the black-backed gulls, which have little to fear, the heron looks cautious even when it is being predatory, its nervousness as useful to it, presumably, as the brashness of the big gulls. Despite its size—adult great blues have seven-foot wingspans—no predatory bird looks more fragile than the great blue heron.

It is impossible to ignore the birds of Mount Desert Island.* The sky here is always busy with flight. Flocks of raucous crows and sometimes small gangs of stiff-winged ravens patrol the rock-rimmed shoreline. The cries of blue jays and calls of kingfishers add character to the busy edge of the spruce-fir woods. Small groups of mallards, flying fast, silently hustle inland toward Bass Harbor Marsh. Gulls, of course, are always coming and going with the intent purposefulness of their kind. Some days, flocks of sandpipers glint over the still water, dodging about wildly en masse, their shimmering flock flight impressive as anything in the air. While I'm watching elsewhere, the heron disappears. I can imagine the deep flex of its long wings, its legs trailing over a blurred impression of itself.

The fog burns off and drifts away, as spring fogs tend to do—not like in late June or July when a dense fog may come to stay, obscuring the summits of Mount Desert's mountains for days or sitting offshore for weeks, making whale watching a game of blindman's bluff. I gather up my few things, sling the pack on my back, and make a way over the cobbles, which clack softly under my weight, to the mouth of Ship Harbor.

The edge of the sea attracts edgy forms of life, one living

---

* If you include rare sightings, there are 357 species on Acadia National Park's bird checklist. Of these, 273 species make regular use of the park's varied habitats.

thing often nested into another—clusters of tiny blue mussels hidden under thick mats of bladder wrack, a cunner fining under a rock in the lower tidal zone. Several species of rockweed lie in inert piles over the broad rim of the upper and mid-tidal zone, while the kelps come to life in the black waters of the lower tidal zone, sharking around in the currents, pivoting on hidden holdfasts.

In a world of so much interdependence, you cannot pick up one thing only—a sugar kelp clings to a half-eaten mussel; a small clam is attached to the horse mussel on which a periwinkle gleans. Along the spring-tide wrack line, the detritus of the great work of fishing tangles itself in artless heaps—lobster buoys, toggles, wrecked traps, spars, and cordage. Some of the latter is too good not to salvage, though I have no other use for it than to hang odd lengths of thick manila rope on the walls of my office at home in central Pennsylvania next to a tidal clock set to the Ship Harbor tide.

Contending forces and strategies of survival are sharply drawn at the edge of the sea, the marine environment as harsh and unforgiving as it is beautiful. In the quiet water where the heron waded, now a cormorant plucks a sculpin from the water beneath it, bringing its luckless prey to the surface crosswise in the implacable grip of its stout bill. Readying the only defense it has—a final gesture, really, given the cormorant's skill—the sculpin fans a threatening array of thick-spined fins. Two ancient instincts are poised against one another for one moment until the cormorant deftly switches its grip to swallow the doomed fish headfirst.

From the Ship Harbor channel, your steps will eventually lead you out to a peninsula that overlooks the eastern approach to Bass Harbor Head, out of sight to the west. There is a well-used trail through the spruce-fir woods, but the best way is to walk the cobble and clamber over the ledge rock and boulders thrown in your way, feel the monumental jumble of this rocky coast in your knees and elbows.

Looking out from this rough-hewn peninsula across the black length of Long Ledge—a narrow shelf of jagged rock at low tide—you can see Little Duck and Great Duck Islands to the south. Great Gott Island lies southwest across the mile of water that separates the Gulf of Maine from Blue Hill Bay, just east of the mouth of Bass Harbor. Just west of Gott, you can see the forested shore of Placentia Island, behind which bits of the long shoreline of Swans Island come in and out of view. The other outer islands that protect Blue Hill Bay from the rougher water of the Gulf lie hidden to seaward—Little Gott and Black Islands behind Great Gott, Green Island, the Sisters, and Long Island, the latter commonly referred to as Frenchboro for the town there.

Any walk along this coastline is a walk through time. This nameless peninsula is the southwestern extremity of Mount Desert Island. The entire tip of the island from Bass Harbor Head to Seawall is sheathed with a fine-grained Devonian granite that is shot through with veins of quartz and feldspar that look like lightning captured by the parent rock. Here and there along the way, you find fragments of Ellsworth Schist, a greenish-grayish metamorphic rock, two billion years old and the oldest building material on Mount Desert.

Hard to say, when scrambling over this pink granite ledge rock etched with bird tracks of fracture and separated into neat blocks by the chemistry and physics of weathering, whether this rocky coast is an image of permanence or impermanence. This granite shore is a paradox. In the middle distance, it seems impregnable; up close, you see how vulnerable it is to the canny, mobile force of the ocean, which patiently gnaws it, coming and going, on every tide. The tiniest vegetation—pioneering mosses, grasses, and wildflowers—will worry apart the same rock out of which monumental buildings in Boston and New York, Chicago and Washington, DC, were fashioned. This relatively young coast is made of ancient material. This appealing dishevelment of boulders broken to bits at the edge of the sea is the work of the hour and a gift of deep time.

Near the woods, a dark realm of spruce and fir, you can move easily from one broad, dry ledge to another, but the closer you get to the tidal zone, the harder the walking goes. In the end, you have to scramble over boulders canted at odd angles, an organized chaos of stonework. Clambering through this landscape, you feel not only physically awkward but psychologically out of place—aesthetically drawn to an environment to which you are not well adapted.

You lower yourself to the mid-tidal zone, where every imaginable size and shape of tidal pool awaits, each a realm of sea life partly rooted there and partly left by chance in the last high tide. Staggering in color and form and dense with a diversity of life, no two tidal pools are the same. They are one of the great gifts of the sea's edge, each a creation of seawater and rock, each a variation on one of nature's finest forms of habitat. You can lose half a day to just one tidal pool if you stop to parse its strange life at low tide or watch one fill by slow degrees as the tide returns.

Stretching around these windows into the evolutionary history of life on earth, you find a long reach of barnacle-encrusted ledge rock exposed by full low tide, a hundred yards or so of magnificent littoral surfaced into view. Walk out on this extremity of Mount Desert when the gulf recedes. Sit behind the outermost ledge so that you are nearly eye level with the sea heaving loudly into the black, wet rocks. Watch the tide swirl in around you by degrees, the trial and error of its advance. Feel the vibration of its insistence—the inanimate necessity of it—in the deep-rooted rock. Hold your place until you are forced to retreat by the tidal flood.

Or come here some evening in midsummer when the sun sets directly behind this reach of land. Come when high tide has completely devoured all this rock, set the rockweed standing and the thousands of barnacles back to feeding, drowned the tidal pools with life-giving salt water, brought the eiders and their new young in close. The setting sun will ease behind the woods, shooting long rays between boles and branches into breaking waves, which palm the cool yellow light into perfect curves. Watch evening come on, those cresting tidal waves curling dusk to darkness like a lathe.

Or come in fall when there is a chill in the air, when you can watch monarch butterflies crossing the Ship Harbor channel beneath gangs of young-of-the-year-laughing gulls. Flocks of sandpipers skid here and there, and occasionally migrating yellowlegs will materialize on mudflats. Raptors move overhead almost constantly—everything driven, it seems, by this metronome of the tide that imposes a cold insistence as autumn foams hurriedly toward winter.

Today at low tide, common eiders hold sway just off the point. Big, stocky sea ducks sturdy as lobster boats, eiders work the shifting near-shore depths to their advantage, diving to feed at will. Strong swimmers, they need that strength to counteract their buoyancy. Eiders are not sleek and oily low-riders like the cormorants that patrol in their vicinity. A diving eider plunges with considerable force into the cold water. If you watch one closely, you will see it hitch and rise before it shoulders itself into the gray chop. You can see the effort it makes to disappear, can feel the difficulty of the plunge, can sense how strong they are. When they are in close and you are standing on one of the broad flat ledges, you can watch the males flashing black and white into the depths. Then they bob to the surface dry as a bone. Or so it seems.

I would apologize for all this bird-watching, but you cannot spend time here and not be drawn to the life of birds. That is something Mount Desert teaches, though I had learned that great lesson elsewhere—on the eastern shore of Virginia and the Outer Banks, in the Blue Ridge and Great Smoky mountains. Small groups of stiff-winged black guillemots fly in and out of view, low to the water. A solitary loon rides the offshore swells, unmistakable in the sleekness of its silhouette. Gulls and seafowl pass at every distance, at every angle. Often there is an eagle or two feasting out on Long Ledge; later in the season, seals will haul out there.

It is probably a fool's errand to try to put too fine a point on what draws us to nature. Our nature draws us to nature, to the edge of the sea. We are, after all, the descendants of tidal creatures. The "subtleness of the sea," Melville notes, would devour and destroy us if we gave it the chance, or—to put it more gently—reform us, change us. Walking, we trend toward edges, our bodies instinctively bringing our minds to places where we might observe and contemplate the keen otherness of nature, that beautiful indifference often revealed at field's edge, or on mountaintops, along rivers, or here, at the edge of the sea—some constantly changing, timeless perfection at work at some border that draws our eye.

Beyond the beauty of nature lies the strangeness of it. In the end, everything at the edge of the sea confirms the hours, tolls their coming and going with the engaged indifference of the Long Ledge bell buoy clanging the period of offshore swells. Walking back through the woods at midday, the birds quiet and the muffled insistence of the tide behind you, you could mistake its tolling for a church bell.

[T]he mountains look like the hulls of capsized ships,
slime-hung and barnacled.

"QUESTIONS OF TRAVEL"

SUMMITS—

Figure and Ground

In late spring, I walk Mount Desert's eastern summits, one by one from east to west, just to stretch my legs on the wild deck of this great ship of rock, just to feel the shape of its whalebacked mountains underfoot. I'll spend a week or so on the slopes of Champlain, Dorr, Cadillac, Pemetic, and Penobscot, saving Sargent Mountain for a long walk on the summer solstice.

On any summit walk, Mount Desert will draw you through its quiet woods and up its gentle, rugged slopes by a kind of capillary action, an attraction of boot soles to rock. The island is scaled perfectly to the theory and practice of walking. It does not surprise me that the art of trail-making was perfected in Acadia National Park and has been thoughtfully practiced on Mount Desert Island since the days when the Penobscot and Passamaquoddy followed unmarked canoe carries through the lowlands between the mountains from one glacial pond to another. Walking will help you get accustomed to the piercing, at times blinding, beauty of the island and will guide you through that beauty toward an instructive familiarity with the lay of the land and the life of things here.

I have learned to set the pace of my walking to the scale of Acadia's well-worn trails. Sense of scale is important on Mount Desert, perhaps the principal art it teaches. None of its historic hiking paths are as long as you would wish. Go too fast—*hike* instead of *walk*—and you will run out of ground for the day, find yourself back at the trailhead in broad daylight rather than moving—owl hoots coming on as doves skid to their roosts—through darkening woods that last half mile to your car.

Ideally, you want to pass the first weathered trail sign when the sky beyond Schoodic Peninsula is still pink with dawn, the lights on Little Cranberry Island still lit, the passing gulls more creatures of the night than birds of the day to come. Then lose yourself on some loop of trails, going slowly enough to catch a sense of the rhythm of the island's fabulous birdlife, the succession of its hardy vegetation, the encouragement of its sweeping views.

Up on Mount Desert's graceful slopes, you can't keep time by the outgoing or incoming wash of tide—as you can when wandering the tidal zone—but you can watch the sun arc resolutely overhead and mark the way the shadows shift from one side of the mountains to the other, as if each long ridge was the gnomon of a great sundial. Or you can sit still and measure an hour by watching birds in the twisted shadows of pitch pines, dense thickets of trees that seem to weave time into knots of living form. Or, walking quietly onward, you can listen, between the crunching of your footsteps, to the seconds ticked by stalks of sandwort rattling in a summit wind.

Walk slowly toward one of the eastern summits, dawdling through the woods on the lower slopes, taking your time on the ledge rock and in the steep places, until it is time to descend again. Lose yourself in a day of being in this landscape until you find yourself coming through some stretch of cool spruce-fir woods growing dark quickly at sunset or, having taken another way, striding through a gentle, burnt-land slope of birch and aspen as the pale trunks of those slender trees give up the light they have held around them since sunrise warmed Schoodic's night-cold granite.

The mountains of Mount Desert Island—really no more than great granite hills—will school you in the art of walking.

Enjoy Champlain Mountain in early June, for example. Wander away from the fading clang of some bell buoy behind you toward the warbler calls in the woods between The Beehive and Gorham Mountain. Move through birch and maple, succulent moosewood. Bunchberry, starflower, sarsaparilla, and common dog violets soften rocky, root-studded ground limned here and there with the rills of intermittent streams that pond in birdy wetlands hidden from view. The nasal slurs of black-throated green warblers, the squeaks of black-and-whites, the rattles of yellow-rumps counterpoint the comic twang of bullfrogs. Listen to the familiar calls of chickadees, mourning doves, and nuthatches and puzzle at the calls and songs you do not know. At every step, you'll sense a stir of life just ahead of you, feel it still as you pass, and then brighten loudly as you move on.

Pass the shallow pond known as The Bowl, a lens of water cupped in granite palms, and its attendant beaver meadows. Pickerel frogs scatter from its outlet stream as you step across the bright rill. An ovenbird, all eye and stillness, takes refuge in blooming rhodora. A trail laced with tree roots becomes a trail of rock. Move up onto the modest southern ridge of Champlain Mountain through stunted, shoulder-high hardwoods and spruce.

There is a little bit of everything where the forest cover thins— stunted red oaks rattling dryly, the chalky leaves of bigtooth aspen swinging wildly on weak stems, dark spruce and fir contrasting with the pale grace of young red maple and white birch, which seem to glow with an inner light. Ferns and wildflowers give way to the mosses, lichens, and ground-hugging herbs that have mined soil out of granite since the glaciers retreated and, relieved of all that weight, the land rose.

Then the foot of Champlain shoulders itself above the forested hem of the island and you scramble up an abrupt incline of weathering boulders onto a broad, well-fissured slab of bare granite picketed by bearberry, blueberry, and pitch pine. You find yourself suddenly among well-weathered Ice Age stonework. A dark-eyed junco probably trills once or twice from within the dark thatch of pitch pine, then seems somehow to disappear, though you have not seen it.

As you stop to catch your breath on the first bare expanse of rock, a sea breeze chills the damp between your shoulder blades. You feel the space behind you, turn around, and realize what you thought you knew—that for every height in this landscape there is a depth, that any walk into these mountains will deepen your subconscious appreciation of the ways the land meets the sea on Mount Desert Island.

From these shelves of rock on Champlain Mountain you see Mount Desert's magnificent southeast headlands from behind, one form of glacial sculpting mirroring another, solemn variations on the theme of granite's resistance to ten thousand years of weather. Enoch Mountain, The Beehive, Halfway Mountain—the names don't much matter, but the fundamental art of this landscape, this play of figure and ground, is the principal reward for walking here. As if this landscape gave you extraordinary power, you easily move through time here, through reciprocal shapes of air, rock, and water, through the accident of a day's weather and the irresistible momentum of an epoch of rocky stasis vibrating faintly with the restless energy of the ocean.

Once you are behind and above the headlands, you get your first views out to open water, good looks south at Baker Island, Sutton Island and the Cranberries, the Duck Islands, and Long Island, where the town of Frenchboro is nestled. You can see west across Blue Hill Bay, so fine for kayaking, all the way to the Camden Hills on the far side of Penobscot Bay. Contemplating these vistas, you sense Mount Desert to be both the center of an impressive archipelago and a landmark on the horizon of other islands.

A little farther on, the trail forces you steeply up and around a large angle of rock. Grabbing for handholds, you feel the cold graininess roughening your fingertips and killing your knees, a short stretch where you have to exert yourself up through the unfinished business of erosion. When you are done with that abrupt pitch and gain the next easy slope of rock, you will wander to the west side of the mountain, following other steps worn faintly across a granite bald to where you can see far—not out but inland.

From there you watch gulls and ravens fly through the unspeakably graceful space between Dorr and Champlain Mountains, the most easterly of the great glacial cirques, those deep bowls of blue air between Mount Desert's whaleback summits that give it such a distinctive profile from the sea—the look that Champlain described in 1604 and that the Puritan leader John Winthrop sketched from the deck of the *Arbella* in 1630 on his way to Salem.

From this vantage, that famous horizon is underfoot. You look north toward Huguenot Head and The Tarn and the steep cliffs of Dorr Mountain, the gentle space of Great Meadow beyond and then the waters of Frenchman Bay and on to a mainland ruffled in places with granite mountains shaped by the weight of the same glaciers that carved and polished the rock ledge at your feet.

Moving north again, up the long, gentle slope of Champlain, you raise more and more of the ocean into view behind you. By the time you get eye level with turkey vultures working weak morning thermals, you see that by walking up Champlain Mountain from the south you are walking, dry shod, to Bar Harbor by way of Frenchman Bay. Champlain Mountain overlooks the mouth of the bay, giving you good looks at Schoodic Mountain and the foaming peninsula seaward of it, as well as the outer passage into Bar Harbor between Turtle Island and Egg Rock, whose weak foghorn you can hear up on Champlain when the wind is right. You can see the well-named Ironbound Island—its bow sheathed in dark columns of basalt—anchored in the middle of the bay as if turned on its cables by a stiff breeze out of the south-

southwest. You see the way the thickly forested Porcupine Islands have arranged themselves to suggest the hard turn to port that brings ships into Bar Harbor. You see the way the broad expanse of upper Frenchman Bay joins Mount Desert Narrows, which barely separates Mount Desert Island from the mainland.

If you spend time on Frenchman Bay, you know that in early June harbor seals haul out on Egg Rock on the falling tides, their dark fur drying pale gray in the sun. Other seals bottle in the lee waters, adults herding the playful young in safe directions. You will have heard seal pups bark pleasantly to the silent, stoic adults—animals that seem to rest uncomfortably on land, stranger than any animal I know in repose.

With those vultures still tilting overhead—some animated and almost hawklike, others wooden and passive on the air—you can watch the tide streaming around Egg Rock, dead center in the mouth of Frenchman Bay, and also remember the eiders nesting there in the tiny island's grasses and on its guano-stained rocks along with herring gulls and black-backed gulls. The prospect of all that helpless unfledged birdlife below keeps raptors on patrol. It is rare to sail out of Bar Harbor and not see a bald eagle perched there or wheeling overhead.

From Champlain, you get good views down at the near shore— a bird's-eye view of Great Head and Schooner Head, of Newport Ledge and Old Whale Ledge, hull-crunching shoal water whitened by all tides. By the time you get to Champlain's summit— an undramatic, cairn-topped rise—you can look down on The Thrumcap, a small, tide-heaved dome of rock where cormorants nest surrounded by some profusely blooming wildflowers.

Stand on Champlain's summit in June, looking inward on the

island and out to sea by turns. Breathe in a primal sense of freedom, feed on well-expressed space, borrow its composure. Feel keenly those ratios of balanced forces and all the earth-shaping work done here slowly by time. Enjoy the airy weight of this landscape.

In part, what you see on any summit walk is an exposed edge of deep time, a stony arrangement of the earth's eons and hours, a momentary expression of the surface of the earth. Seated on a comfortable ledge to eat or rest, you look down and notice the broken rock at your feet, casually study the way granite fractures neatly, quarrying itself into blocks, shelf rock exfoliating in thick sheets, boulders spalling miniature replicas of themselves. On the summits, it's as if the earth were slowly molting—shedding skin—which of course it is.

Sometimes you notice a tip of rock calved off the edge of an outcrop, cleaved just the previous winter perhaps by a thin chisel of ice, cut neatly as a piece of cake. You can imagine the quiet *chink* when it fell, distinct as a junco's call note. And you notice the fragment is shaped like its parent rock and that the parent rock is shaped like the ridge you are walking up and that the ridge is shaped like the mountain, which in turn shapes the air and the sea around it. And you wonder, as you pack up to move on, what the parent of these well-shaped hours is, what expresses itself here in all this granite curved as gracefully as gull wings.

⑥

A few days later, in early June, I'll head for the summit of Dorr. I'll cross the marshy outlet wetlands of The Tarn on the Canon

Brook Trail, spooking painted turtles off logs as hairy woodpeckers slowly probe wet birch. These are the lowlands I saw from up on Champlain, the narrow, southern end of that perfect glacial bowl. A small, ragged stream bogs down in a series of beaver ponds and overflow, a meander of spring runoff with so few contour lines left between it and the sea that its dark water bulges and seeps rather than flows from one to the next.

Looking up at the steep slopes of Huguenot Head and Champlain to check the progress of a waning fog, I feel very much at the bottom of something, which I am, since I'm traversing the space left by the retreat of a glacier ten thousand years ago. You can sense the weight of that ice in the space and feel the time, not much by geological standards, since this valley was formed. This small drainage, half-hidden between the bases of Champlain and Dorr Mountains, is barely above sea level. The brimming gulf and the weight of the ocean bides its time just beyond the mouth of Otter Cove. In fact, all the island's glacial valleys are nearly cut to sea level, each almost a bay of the waiting gulf—like Somes Sound. In fact, the clays and silts in this freshwater wetland are of marine origin, laid down when a sheltered arm of the sea reached inland to the foot of Huguenot Head.

I could spend a day here, and I have, but I move on with the itch to cover ground and get up on the cool, blue moody summits. I walk through half-open woods, skirting the forested base of Dorr Mountain, and then cross the foot of it until I'm stopped again by water—this time not the inky stillness of a wetland but the clatter of a running stream.

The A. Murray Young Path heads up along Otter Creek, which is a textbook study in streambed formation, a bright cascade slowly abrading mossy rock ledges to its purposes, the high energy of falling water breaking down rock to create low-energy niches. Up here, as in the tidal zone, fluidity eventually wins out over resistance. Small white tributaries crackle off the steep slopes on either side, all this stream sound echoing down the rocky mountainsides, blending with the cry and response of birdlife. All along this way, you walk steeply up stonework steps so old they seem now to be a natural part of the mountain, the well-crafted artifice of one of Acadia's famous old paths, carved out of the mountain in the 1920s when such monumental trail-work was in fashion.

The steep crease between Champlain and Dorr narrows as you ascend to the saddle that joins the two mountains. Yellow birch appear at some contour to their liking, and where the soil thins and sunlight broadens its reach, gray birch mark the way. At some point, though still in the woods, you feel that you are getting up into another realm, becoming a creature of granite rather than a creature of spruce-fir.

Perhaps you feel the change where you start catching a sea breeze, great gouts of cool air from the Gulf of Maine drifting inland. As you move up this narrow way, you gain sky and start to get close looks at the eastern flank of Cadillac, a great piece of coastal stonework from any angle. Turning around to find the warblers that announce this higher terrain, you catch a glimpse of the ocean, which will remain a distraction for the rest of the day. With thrush calling below you and a woodpecker *cacking* in the woods you are leaving behind, you take a few more steps and the effort raises Otter Cove into view. As you continue to ascend, the gulf appears over the treetops below you, and from this new perspective there is an illusion that the sea is high enough to flood the valley below, that the next high tide will occupy the way came.

This trail brings you underneath a brow of Cadillac thinly guarded by scraggly red pine. At one point you feel a wonderful blast of cool air from out of the mountain near the streambed— a spring source perhaps, a cave where the gods store wind and water. In some places you can hear a rill of a stream underneath you, the head of Otter Creek flowing inside the mountain.

Then you have to stow your binoculars, notes, and water in the day pack and scramble through the jumble of a debris field that forms the crumbling saddle between Cadillac and Dorr, a chaos of boulders and scree that looks as if it might have rumbled into place the night before.

This progress moves a great swath of the horizon behind you. You can see sunlight glinting off the windshields of lobster boats bobbing at their work, the white rustle of the tide around ledge rock and headlands. The cool ocean looks good from up on these hot rocks where late spring simmers toward summer. In the end, there is no trail except a body-width of passage through the jammed weight of that silent, monumental scree. You climb up through it, feeling as if you are being handed from rock to rock, and come to one of the island's great trail crossings, the nexus of many good walks you can take on this part of the island.

You turn east, onto the Cadillac–Dorr Trail, climb a short, steep pitch of bare rock, and then cruise through a cool tunnel of pitch pine. Juncos rattle, white-throats call from somewhere, occasionally a yellow-rumped or black-throated green warbler will swoop across your field of vision. When you get there, the summit of Dorr, like the crest of all of Acadia's peaks, is a satisfying anticlimax. You are rewarded with breathtaking space and a familiar vista—Frenchman Bay, Bar Harbor, Schoodic Peninsula, and the coast east toward Petit Manan, the open gulf to the south, the scatter of islands to the southwest.

All walks in these Acadian highlands are variations on a great untitled theme, the work in progress of this broad, unfathomable landscape. Come to Mount Desert year after year. Walk incessantly, as I and many others do and have done for 150 years. You will never get to the bottom of these summits, never tire of the routine of spending mornings in woods full of birds, afternoons in a world of granite and sky, looking out and looking down, every hour informed by the influence of the nearby sea. You will never tire of descending those granite slopes, step by satisfying step, and reentering the lowland woods.

Take the long South Ridge Trail up Cadillac Mountain. Walk through thickly shadowed spruce woods on a trail that doubles in places as a streambed and that in mid-June will be awash in pollen. Let the traffic from Route 3 be erased by the calls of nuthatches, black-and-white warblers, mourning doves, bay-breasted warblers, black-throated green warblers, blue jays, woodpeckers, ovenbirds, and who knows what else.

Read the sound-absorbing understory of the spruce woods as you go: granite boulders sheathed in thick moss mats, profusions of wild ferns and ground yews, textbook displays of polyphores—shelf fungi—on the trunks of living and dead trees. Note an enormous, ancient white birch rotting away in the cool shade of the spruce that succeeded it.

Eventually spruce gives way to pine, as it does on every southern exposure. Watch the dense woods open into small granite balds where low-bush blueberry suns itself. Feel an earthen trail become a faintly worn path on bedrock; watch the trees shrink to shoulder level. Stunted pines make way for wiry heaths rooted in fissures and small islands of soil. Then pass through a wandering treeline above which there are mostly dry, sun-blanched granite shelves, broad staircases of ledge rock that support only grasses and wildflowers, tiny leather-leaved herbs, and blooms of lichens.

Going up Cadillac, let yourself be distracted by the rock outcropping known as Eagles Crag, a good vantage from which to watch a distant morning fog dissipate. Take your time moving through a notable stand of jack pine—one of the hardiest northern pines—another half mile up the trail. When you reach an unnamed pond and wetland, stop to admire the unspeakably beautiful shape of the interior of the island, its glacial sculpting, the play of foreground, middle distance, and horizon that seems to embody motion in its well-formed stillness.

From each of Mount Desert's modest summits, the idea of land answers the idea of water brilliantly. Heights and depths, headlands and coves, the intimate recesses of mossy rock at your feet and a limitless horizon in your eye. The fundamental cry and response in the landscape rings clear at every step. You can contemplate the mobility of a peregrine falcon or the perfect stasis of a pitch pine.

Move slowly, stop often. Practice forms of patience that the busy world defeats at every turn—observe, think, feel, loaf. Enjoy space and silence, form and color, your own vigor and fatigue, unaccountable fits of boredom as well as moments of keen awareness when the life of things seems to be a part of your own life, moments when the landscape seems to ride easily on your shoulders, the weight of the world a pleasure to bear. Observe, recognize, conjecture, speculate, understand, know. Open your senses and your mind to the nature of things. If you have the appetite for it, learn the names of whatever interests you, find words as you walk, sentences, lines of verse that run on or enjamb. Become privy to an epic dialogue of spare elements lavishly arranged on the summits of Mount Desert Island—a wordless colloquy here to be overheard on any day, in any season, in any weather.

In the *Timaeus*, Plato reasons that nature is an expression of intelligence and necessity. He speculates that the four elements—so graphically displayed here on Mount Desert at every turn—nursed becoming into being in the natural interest of making order out of chaos. I don't follow Plato and a long succession of others in seeing some divine authorship at work in this, but the inherent intelligence and necessity in things seems clear—that rock desires to be rock; air, air; water, water; fire—the energy in things—fire.

Clearly everything that is, animate and inanimate, desires to be and aspires in place by adaptations the forms and strategies of which we recognize only in retrospect, since—evolution teaches us—unsuccessful adaptations disappear, usually without a trace. There are, after all, many things we only understand this way, in retrospect, many forms and patterns in nature we only come to appreciate over time.

Such thinking is not far-fetched here. It's worth remembering that Western philosophy arose and evolved at the edge of the sea, in Asia Minor, and on bare summits like these. The rocky coast and islands of the Aegean invited observation and made space for thought, giving us the Ionians, Thales and Anaximander of Miletus, Heraclitus, Pythagoras, and the other pre-Socratics who had no school but nature itself. I've met more than a few people—none of them philosophers—who have told me that their two favorite places to sail are the Greek isles and the coast of Maine.

We don't need to split hairs with Socrates and Plato, but when you get away from the recreational clamor of Mount Desert—which can become quite discouraging at times—these spare granite foregrounds and long seaward views will pleasantly draw you inward and outward leaving you with the need to make connections. Walking, after all, invites observation and stimulates thought, but creates more questions than answers. *What is that?* For those of us who love the outdoors, the rhythm of walking underwrites the unassuming narrative of our coming to understand the places we love—or at least to appreciate them—the landscapes we try to inhabit in our minds. Of course, in the end, there is no need to reason your way to the beauty you find in store for you on Mount Desert Island. Walk, observe, enjoy. See what you can see.

No one can walk these summits without becoming attached to the austere company of pitch pines, which come into their glory on these sun-drenched, windswept granite balds. *Pinus rigida* is a humble tree in most landscapes in the East, a weed tree to many, though I would never consider it such. On Mount Desert it grows where few other trees will or can and where heaths or even more modest vegetation would easily take over.

It is the genius of pitch pine to root in rock and branch in air, twisting itself toward soil and light, creating beautiful, imaginative form out of sheer necessity. Roots root, branches branch. Is it botany or language that drives such growth toward the perfectly irregular balance of its form? This humble, common tree seems to be simultaneously an embodiment and a transcendence of the beautiful truth in all things, beauty being perhaps the form of any successful evolution, any successful persistence in time.

These Acadian summits are a complement to Mount Desert's restless tidal zones and quiet woods. They offer another way of spending time with the nature of nature. Like the tidal zones and the island's forested interior, the summits are spare and lavish, simple and complex, inviting and off-putting. Walking across these granite domes, enjoying spacious hours, you will feel keenly related to the sky and to the sea, to the rock underfoot and to the life of things here.

Some days, walking Acadian summits, soaking up the informed silence of these mountains, you'll want to bow to everything you see.

The whole coast along here is iron bound—threatening crags, and dark caverns in which the sea thunders.

—THOMAS COLE

IRONBOUND COAST—

Land Partly at Sea

Nature is not intentionally theatrical. The drama we sometimes see in landscapes is a projection of something in us, the trace of a nagging fear that we do not belong in nature, that we are no match for the forces that brought us into being. Violent weather revives in us an ancient capacity for awe and a humility when confronting the nature of things that was once our principal evolutionary advantage. When we come face to face with the blunt force of the world, fear, awe and humility are a good way to start.

Mount Desert Island seems underfit to its surroundings in fair weather, small for the space it occupies, shrunk behind placid ledges to a safe distance from the profound energy of the Gulf of Maine, its rocky margins withdrawn on fair days from full contact with the sea. Except for strong spring tides—which in places leave the damp tangle of their wrack lines at the edge of the woods—the great fetch of open water stretching south from Mount Desert toward Georges Bank and the true, abyssal Atlantic can be as placid as a field, as two-dimensional as a postcard. In summer especially, when the coast is harried by traffic and obscured by thronging crowds, this great coastal exposure can seem like no big deal, the work of lobstermen moving easily from trap to trap, labor anyone could do.

Storms enlarge the island. Heavy seas lean toward the shore, overriding the tidal zones with swollen depths of gray seawater that refuses to recede for a day or so. The risen sea imposes a massive buoyancy around Mount Desert's margins—a pounding flood tide that would not so much drown the island as carry it off. Thick ranks of frothy rollers thrum on the coastal bedrock, reaching boldly around and under it, threatening to free the great rock hull from its ways, release the island for adventure. Headlands plow forward, taking stone sails of mountains with them. A lowering sky thick with granite clouds brings to life the resiliency of the tall coastal conifers, mast wood that breaks but does not bend, standing until it shatters, spiked to its heartwood, sea torn.

Mount Desert moves in storms, rising and falling, absorbing as much of the sea's energy as it can and shedding the rest through scuppers of weedy rock. Get out on that great seaward-facing stonework from Great Head to Hunters Point in a fall nor'easter and the mainland will seem a hundred miles away. The island will lean on a hidden keel into the authority of a wind you will bow down to in order not to be blown over. Birds are my most reliable guides to everything here, but except for a few mad gulls, even they disappear in storms, awed.

I'm at Little Hunters Beach, eye level with an early October storm surge, listening to the wind and the ocean roar into the rocks. Under the influence of a little bad weather, the island's seaward edge has come to life. A sullen low slowly passing offshore has got a twelve-foot sea running in front of an east-southeast wind that blew hard during the night and has been slowly gusting itself out all morning. I've been making my rounds in the rain on the Park Loop Road, stopping here and there to admire the way the island goes to sea.

By the time I get to Little Hunters Beach, the rain is tapering off, but the wind is still up and the sea running hard. The incoming tide will have an authority worth watching for an afternoon.

The southeast shore of Mount Desert Island, considered by some to be the aesthetic climax of the coast of Maine, is sheathed in a band of shatter-zone rock, a monumental, dark jumble of volcanic boulder work of varied origin that abuts the famous pink Devonian granite exposed in the island's eastern summits. Little Hunters Beach is a pronounced rectangular notch in the coast between Western Point and Hunters Head, a failure of that shatter-zone bulwark into which the sea dead-ends in a strand of cobbles, a clutch of strange stone eggs that clack ominously in strong tides.

In bad weather, the sea dead-ends loudly here, doubling back on itself in a welter of standing waves, bursting white into the gray air but black beneath the froth, with the dark confusion of a running sea trapped in a granite cul-de-sac. When you stand on those cobbles in a storm, the incoming tide seems to come in head-high or higher. Watching there, you will be looking into the sea rather than at it, a roiled brow of water with the authority of the ocean behind it coming toward you. You will understand that between the roar of breakers on the cliffs, the mutter of spent waves clawing the air in every direction, and the clatter of those cobbles in the black fist of the tide, the voice of the sea—its "fumbling, deep-structured roar," as James Dickey once put it—is no cliché. The elements speak, when roused, and we are free to listen to the din. There is not much in culture—in art—that can stand up to the sea. One thinks of Prospero and Odysseus or of Yeats's Cuchulain, sword in hand, or those wild conversations between Ahab and Starbuck that Ishmael reports to us in Melville's great book.

When you get tired of facing the dark roar of the ocean directly, the rugged point just east of Little Hunters Beach is a good vantage for watching this coast in a storm. From there you can see other islands riding the gray weather—Schoodic far off to the east, getting badly beaten; Baker to the south; the foaming mess of the Bunker Ledges; and then, looking west, Sutton and the Cranberry Isles, which mark the way toward the mouth of Somes Sound. Familiar shapes, the nearer islands are domestic places you can reach by kayak on a fair day. In bad weather, they seem like distant and dismal destinations.

In rough weather, the outer islands are merely forested volcanic rock fringed with storm surf, more shatter-zone debris like the bony, tilted ledge on which I'm trying to get comfortable, rock that hasn't weathered smooth like granite but just flakes into newly sharp edges, as inhospitable as the original shards of whatever eruption put it here.

Storm-watching is an art. Here the trick is to get in the lee of a gnarled spruce, the last windbreak on this unnamed headland. You can hear the roar of the breakers exploding on the granite walls of Little Hunters Beach, which is behind you now. And above that fray you can still hear the distinct rattling of the cobbles under the white wash of a storm surge, aided by the incoming tide hidden within the energy of this passing rough weather. That angry chant of wet stones is at least a hundred yards away, but somehow the gusting wind makes it seem that the stony, wet clatter is inside your head.

Once you've settled down to watch, rain gear toggled tight, you get a sense that despite the din and visual confusion, any sensible animal can wait out any storm. The strong gusting winds driving off the gulf pin you against your niche in the rocks, their force disappearing into the spruce-fir woods behind you. Maritime forests absorb the energy and effects of rough weather with admirable ease, the dense, diverse vegetation shedding water a thousand ways. The hoary white spruce common here rummage about in place, birch leaves flicker, purple asters quiver at your feet.

Due to the steep pitch of this ragged brow of rock, the tidal zones here are short and deep. You look into a surging, dark weight of water that keeps thick colonies of rockweed standing in the relentless double flow of breakers overriding the incoming tide. And you see the genius of rockweed fully revealed. Naturally torn, and ribbed to twist their rubbery fronds, the rockweeds fend off the energy of the crashing surf so deftly that they easily survive the worst storms with no more harm than a good pruning of their weakest members. When it is done with the rockweed zone, the incoming sea gnaws at the band of gray barnacles, which have—like the rock to which they have fastened themselves—evolved to rely on the advantage of unyielding resistance.

Storms test what things are, the ways in which life has taken its chances at the edge of the sea, test the strategies of seaside evolution as harshly as they have tried the aspirations of human economy on this coast. An important part of the ecology of any island, storms impose limits.

Two hours after the tide turns, the rain stops but the gulf swells, its great counterclockwise gyre driven directly onto this southern exposure. In storms, it's as if the wind has driven the horizon into the foreground. The effect is intimidating, an epic foreshortening of landscape in the face of weather. The tide pounds white on the rocks all up and down the coast as far as you can see, flowing into tidal pools at your feet in the haunting way that tides progress, advancing in a thousand retreats. Somehow the sea keeps coming in and somehow the island won't move.

As the tide rises, the steep, jagged walls of tidal-zone rock shed white manes of cold seawater, glisten black and green, bubbling with air for a moment, and then disappear under the next surge. You see the canniness, the unnamable design in the calculus of water occupying unyielding space. But the space does yield. In storms you see that, in the long run, water shreds rock more successfully than rock shreds water. Like some great mythic persona, water regathers itself, easily becomes whole again as rock cannot.

Mount Desert Island itself seems whole again in storms, come fully to life as a wild, natural place—not a tourist destination but a primal shard of nature. A day or two of storm surge seems to erase the encroachment of development and tourism, undoes for a few hours the domesticity of culture and takes us back in time, revealing natural energies at their great work.

Storms restore the natural dignity of this coast, that primal otherness hidden everywhere in nature. Storms replace placid beauty with what used to be called the sublime. The power of storms brings us back to a threshold of mythic awareness. Even the island's natives, who have seen their share of weather, come out for storm-watching.

But if storms bring the oceanic horizon into the foreground— shove a great unknown in your face—nothing is revealed by that proximity. Storms are a primitive *cri de coeur*, the barbaric yawp of the earth itself, a howling. They carry no message and do not inspire epiphanies. They restore us to a condition of awe. At the edge of the sea, storms remind us that, on this planet, land is the exception and not the rule.

When the rain eases, I bring out my 15x binoculars and a spotting scope, both waterproof and worth the extra cost of that. I'm keeping an eye out for seabirds that might have come inshore with the weather, maybe storm-petrels, shearwaters, and gannets— unusual to see from shore—steering around this low. Since this is early October, I'm also watching for scoters—called "coots" Down East—which appear here in numbers in the fall and signal an important turn in the year that will climax, in winter, with the appearance of king eiders, red-throated loons, and other High Arctic species come south for the relative hospitality of Maine waters in December and January.

The numbers of resident common eiders are beginning to

swell with migrants from the north, a population that moves down from the Canadian Maritimes to winter here. These birds, done fledging this year's young along the coast of Labrador, Newfoundland, and Nova Scotia, do not bring the cold with them—fall is often warm on the coast—but they do herald the colder half of the year, a long season of shorter days that makes you regret squandering the surfeit of summer daylight.

Except for watching the strong tide, the day comes to be about watching eiders—the singular fact of each stocky, buoyant bird as well as the seasonal story implied by the long rafts of hundreds of them becoming thousands of them in early autumn. The long, loose strands of male eiders, mature and immature birds, flash in the roll of the waves and wink in and out of view as they dive and surface, feeding for mollusks just off the rocks. They feed just beyond the breakers, diving singly or en masse into the gray swells. More often than not, they pop back to the surface, quivering something down their throat or holding a crab gingerly.

A century ago, eiders were on the brink of extirpation on this coast—prized for the down that keeps them warm through wet, frigid winters and with which they line their nests in spring. In 1905 there was reported to be only one nesting pair on the entire coast of Maine. A little wisdom and forbearance gave North Atlantic eider populations enough of a break to enable them to rebreed themselves back into view, affording us another opportunity to observe what eiders are. Now the southernmost population of common eiders—*Somateria mollissima dresseri*—thrives on the Gulf of Maine.

The eiders feed with increasing enthusiasm at half-tide,

perhaps when some favored food is at an ideal depth or density. Despite the roughness of the near-shore water, a good thirty yards of jostling waves, most of the eiders want to be over the lower tidal zone as the mid-tidal zone is being flooded by the incoming tide. When a wave curls prematurely and threatens to break over them, they dive in a line to get under the force of it. Each big duck disappears under itself, leaving a small boil on the surface and then a gray smudge in the gray water. Whole groups disappear at once, perhaps to herd prey and improve their chances at capturing whatever moves in the dark water. Gulls hang in the air, ready to scavenge this work, while cormorants feed in the nervous water at the edges of these big flocks of eiders.

As conditions improve, I start to see mature and immature guillemots and, farther out, loons bobbing in and out of view on swells so deep it takes seconds for one to return into view. Then I finally see the scoters I'd been looking for—white-winged scoters—easily distinguishable at a distance. These are the first scoters I have seen this season—a half dozen quartering into the wind headed west out at the loons' range. They form a ragged line close to the water, flying with a slower wingbeat than hurrying eiders. They seem to struggle to contain their agility and fidget up and down a bit in formation as they hustle along.

White-winged scoters are a sign of autumn and a good-enough culmination to my storm-watching, the last of an afternoon of rewards. The species breeds mostly on forested northern lakes but also on river deltas and tundra from North Dakota through western Canada and into Alaska, from the Aleutians to the North Slope. Along with surf scoters and black scoters, which also come to winter here, the white-wings are especially numerous during breeding season—late spring and early autumn—between Great Slave Lake and the Arctic Ocean.

Although they look quite at home on the coast of Maine, scoters are creatures of the western sub-Arctic and western Arctic. They know good places to breed in the Northwest Territories— the Slave River Delta, the Mackenzie River Delta, Old Crow Flats. They know Yellowknife. In Alaska, scoters breed on the Yukon Flats, in the Tanana-Kuskokwim Valleys, along the coast from Bristol Bay to Kotzebue Sound, and in the Selawik marshes. White-wings have been observed offshore of St. Lawrence Island, in the Endicott Mountains, and along Alaska's Arctic coast. Some winter on the Pacific coast, but a large number return to the Atlantic flyway. To see scoters appear off Mount Desert Island on an early October afternoon is to see summer end in the Arctic.

Suddenly there are more gulls in the air, flying east and west. The scoters are long gone and I've lost the loons. Cormorants darkly arrow by with a wingbeat of their own, a graceful stroke, quick but not hurried. Now and then, without any apparent reason, a herring gull will give out a braying call. Perhaps it's just all the energy in the air. Shafts of sunlight break through in the west, turning a distant patch of gray water silver, a detail that is almost too painterly, too suggestive of some revelation beyond the way things are here as rough seas settle down. A far-off laughing gull looks like a tern in the silver light. I hear crows in the dripping woods behind me. A dragonfly absurdly darts out over the rocks, and I notice the purple asters again.

The tide is now up on the highest ledges, flooding the uppermost tidal pools, which don't refresh on every tide. I keep looking for seabirds—at least the flitter of a storm-petrel—but find none. The coast looks exhausted, rock and water, but that is probably only my fatigue. I'm tired of watching but don't want to leave. Under the magnification of the spotting scope, the gray sea turns to stone.

So there is no earthly way of finding out precisely what the whale really looks like.

—HERMAN MELVILLE,
MOBY-DICK

SURFACINGS —

The Color of the Sea

Finback whales surface without much fanfare. What for whale-watchers is a dramatic event is to this great animal merely a matter of drawing breath. We know that, of course, but the sight of any whale still stirs the imagination, as if that strange gray bulk of marine life hungry for the same air we breathe suddenly made us intimate with everything we don't know about the ocean. If anything on earth knows what the ocean is, whales know. We can only watch with envy when they rise to breathe in sight of us.

The first and largest finback whale I have ever seen surfaced out of a calm, befogged sea twenty miles or so off Mount Desert Island late one raw June day. In fog you don't watch for whales, you listen for them. You lean on a wet railing rather than hang onto sodden rigging, but you are not much different in the way you slowly cock your head about than a Basque sailor, wool cap snug to his skull, listening for a blow five centuries ago. Good whalers, like good whale researchers, knew the sounds of every species they sought and could parse subtle differences in tone, duration, and volume like a birder differentiating bird calls in the woods. To an experienced ear, a finback no more sounds like a humpback than a red-eyed vireo sounds like a solitary vireo.

The unexpected reward for five hours of blind listening, this finback announced itself visually, suddenly appearing in the smoky water not more than a hundred feet off the port side of the idling ship. Its great head and tail remained hidden, but forty feet of gray whaleback arced by with a slow rush of sound barely distinguishable from the quiet wash of the gulf's gray water on the hull below me. The whale must have blown right there alongside us, but even after all that waiting, I do not particularly remember the sound or sight of that. You instinctively hold your breath in the presence of whales. Their broad backs part the grayness of the sea, time arching almost to a stop, until they plunge forward and out of sight at some profound, oceanic pace, the casual rhythm of cetacean travel.

That day, like everyone else on board, I had given up any expectation of seeing a whale. But I take whale-watch boats out of Bar Harbor mostly to see pelagic birds. I had seen Wilson's storm-petrels hanging off the stern of the ship a few times, small flocks of gulls and terns gathered over disturbances of baitfish here and there, even a passing shearwater or two. Sometimes the fog thinned enough to reveal solitary gray seals and pods of passing porpoises, sea-colored marine life momentarily visible a few hundred yards out. Occasionally an immature gannet flew in and out of view with a stoic look of long-distance travel in its wingbeat.

I am as interested as anyone in watching whales, but a whale-less outing would mean a voucher for another trip, a minor form of piracy on my part, another chance at seeing whales and off-shore birds. Near the end of any whale-less excursion, I secretly root for whales to elude us. No day on Gulf of Maine waters is uneventful. I'll take any opportunity to watch the restless, cor-rugated surface of the sea, an ecologically complicated terrain, if you will, for which we landlubbers have little language. Waves and currents, after all, govern most of the surface of the earth. And fog, which encourages stillness and listening, is a frequent companion on the coast of Maine, an important part of its weather and ecology. And in fog, you feel truly at sea. Twenty miles off the coast, you might be anywhere.

When whales are not showing themselves, life is all around, if mostly hidden under your hull. Despite daunting environmen-tal problems, including tragic and shortsighted overfishing, the waters off Mount Desert Island are rich with life. The Census of Marine Life for these waters, a work-in-progress, listed 3,317 spe-cies at the beginning of 2006—652 species of fish, 184 species of birds, 32 species of mammals and thousands of species of inverte-brates and plant life. The ecology of the Gulf of Maine entertains a spectrum of life that ranges in size from microscopic diatoms and dinoflagellates to blue whales, the largest animals on earth.

Despite ongoing concern about remnant whale populations—especially that of the rare (about 350 individuals) right whale—and about the decimation of groundfish stocks, science continues to find new forms of life in the gulf, including fourteen species of deepwater coral.

You can't *see* all this biological diversity, of course, but any day out on the gulf can be a thought experiment in appreciating this complex web of marine life, a wealth of evolutionary success that still persists between the coast of Maine and Georges Bank. Part of the significance of whales is that as apex predators they gather much of this life into view, literally bringing to light a large part of gulf ecology when they surface.

So I didn't mind the fog that June day, and I wasn't disappointed with a slowly paced day of fieldwork on open water. Up on Mount Desert's granite slopes, sitting on some rocky peninsula, or offshore, waiting in the fog demands a kind of *practice*, in the Zen sense, a pleasantly formal way of spending time, an unaffected discipline that schools patience and attentiveness. Fog stops us in our tracks, and it was pleasantly eerie the way the large whale-watch catamaran just bobbed about in the mist, engines throbbing. There was nothing else to do but filter out the rhythmic sound of waves on the hull and listen for the breath of a whale. I remember the collective patience of the small, off-season group on board and how, although no one commented on it, we grew a little bit proud of our odd venture. The captain and crew watched us carefully, to see how long paying customers were willing to put up with uneventful, foggy waiting. But the fog was a perfect setting for thoughtful expectation. Everyone seemed to sense what the naturalist's talk implied—that it was a privilege, an extraordinary privilege, to wait in the fog and listen for a whale.

I don't know how my shipmates felt, but when that finback finally appeared beside us, I felt profoundly unprepared to see it for what it was. Like the word *dinosaur,* it's hard to take the word *whale* seriously—partly because of the animal's size, partly because of its powerful mobility, and partly because of something difficult to name. Suddenly being in the presence of a whale doesn't demystify the strangeness of the word. Like *bear* or *wolf, falcon* or *trout,* the tame nouns we have fashioned for wild animals seem—encouraged by the sudden appearance of their referents—inadequate to the living energy and perfect form of the thing itself. At such times, nature surpasses the grammar of our expectations.

What are we supposed to do with the whales we see? How am I supposed to take in a finback surfacing in the fog? I remember the whale's great back and the dorsal fin for which it is named. I remember that, once in view, the brief presence of the whale was uncanny, the animal simultaneously familiar and strange. But I really remember an image more than details, a memory of a memory, a great arc of life the color of the sea.

Judging the enormous whole from the part you see, you imagine the incomparable size of a finback whale and—harder still, its true shape, its living form—the paradox Ishmael puzzled over on Melville's behalf. And you remember your disappointment as it slid powerfully away, not sinking but swimming, leaving long footprints on the surface of the water, distinctly ponded ovals of flat water created by its flukes, prints that, bloom by bloom, show the path of a whale swimming away, a path as distinct, once you have learned to see it, as bear tracks on a riverbank.

Then you have *seen* a whale, been vaguely brushed by its distinct presence, but know in your heart and gut that you need to start over and see another. You weren't ready to take it in. And since you are neither hunting whales for profit nor studying them, the pretext of your gawking is pretty thin, your innocence as a whale-watcher tainted with the centuries of slaughter on which your own world was built and only slightly allied to the scientific effort to understand what whales are before they disappear— not from view on a given day but, one worries, from the earth forever.

Wild animals are representative of the otherness we seek in nature—or that sometimes exposes itself without our seeking it. When we are suddenly in the presence of that otherness, our expectations are defeated, not fulfilled. The appearance of the whale, superficially exciting, was the end of one kind of waiting and the beginning of another. I've felt this way when pursuing bears and wolves in the wild or walking about my woods in Pennsylvania counting coup on ruffed grouse in winter and surveying timber rattlers in summer. Encounters with what is left of wild life offer us glimpses of pure, practical being, *bios* expressing itself in the keenness of successful species that persist in spite of us—whalelike, wolfish, bearish, gallinaceous, reptilian forms of biological genius. These dramatic exposures to other forms of life that, over evolutionary time, have found a way for themselves blinds us as it sheds light on our secret, subconscious discontent at no longer being such a pure part of nature, perfectly instinctive, singularly aware. Whales, after all, don't go about looking for us, any more than bears or wolves or rattlesnakes do. When such creatures find themselves in our presence, they finish what they are doing and disappear. In their sudden absence, we feel the cost of our cultural evolution, our distance and separateness from nature.

A surfacing whale chides our expectations, gives us more than we were watching for, and suddenly puts our sense of life in the context of an otherness too large, too different, and too self-contained—perfectly itself—for us to comprehend without a tectonic shift in our own self-image. Which is perhaps why, consciously or unconsciously, we go out looking for them.

That finback surfaced a few more times. The captain followed without chasing it, keeping the whale in view until it sounded for its terminal dive. In the precious seconds you have with a surfacing whale, you feel your mind fumbling to take in a unique challenge to the eye and mind. Early in their natural history, whales evolved to great size partly because they adapted to a plentiful food source and partly because the buoyancy of saltwater freed their skeletons from the stress of gravity. They live, quite literally, in another world, with a sense of time and space and of the seasons so different from our own that they might as well have formed their consciousness on another planet. When a whale surfaces, it is returning fifty million years to what it was when it lived as an air-breathing land creature along the muddy embayments of Eocene rivers. The size of whales, so impressive to us, means nothing to them. The sea carries their great weight, like a favor in a myth. As repayment, whales reify the ocean, gathering the amplitude of its resources into a living, breathing thing.

When a whale surfaces or breaches near us, we see two things we rarely see—enormous grace and profound originality. The finback I saw sliding by that raw June afternoon off the coast of Mount Desert Island was estimated to be sixty-five feet long—fifty tons of life sleek and powerful enough for oceanic travel, hardy enough for the weather of the North Atlantic, intelligent enough to communicate and behave cooperatively with its fellows, experienced enough to follow its food sources, hopeful enough to breed and birth and nurse its young where they might safely thrive, to take them to be wherever they need to be to become whales.

Although much harmed by whaling in past centuries, whales are as wild and unassailable in spirit as any animal we might encounter, if no wilder, in principle, than the monarch butterflies I have seen far offshore in the fall paddling their delicate wings with odd composure over the same long stretches of open water that bring whales back to their breeding and calving grounds.

Finbacks are common off Mount Desert in summer. They feed opportunistically, on the surface or at depth, on krill, capelin, sand lance, herring, and squid. Each adult finback needs to strain between one and three tons of such prey in its baleen every day in order to maintain its weight. A creature largely of the continental shelf, the finback routinely dives to 650 feet below the surface of the sea, though it can dive deeper, cruises at three to five miles an hour, and can quickly disappear from view with sprints of up to twenty-five mph. Left to enjoy a normal life cycle, fins live ninety to a hundred years. One Antarctic elder lived to 111.

Like crows and coyotes, finbacks express themselves, though the unaided human ear, which does not detect sound waves below whales. In a sense, whales are as common as white-throated sparrows in summer. We need to see whales often enough until they become uncommon in our minds and a truer sense of their rarity emerges. Then we are getting somewhere in our whale-watching, when our *ooh*s and *aah*s settle down into an instructed silence.

The whales we watch are the descendants of terrestrial mammals that had adapted, in part at least, to an aquatic, possibly amphibious, fish-eating existence in the Eocene. They may have bred on land, like seals, but they had begun to exploit food-rich marine environments. These ancient protocetids took the skeleton, limbs, musculature, organs, and dentition of land vertebrates into coastal salt water. These ancestral whales were still relatively small, less than ten feet long, still had molars in their jaws and the pelvis of walking creatures. The principal paleontological specimen of this group, *Pakicetus*, was found in river mud in Pakistan, alongside the remains of land mammals. The evolution of whales represents, literally, what the ocean has done with a terrestrial idea. Whales are the ultimate result—in size, intelligence, and complexity of behavior—of the genius of the land taking its chances with the genius of the sea.

Modern whales, the toothed and baleen whales we see in the Gulf of Maine today, apparently evolved from a common ancestor—a descendant of those toothy protocetids—and became distinct from one another by the early Oligocene. The odontocetes, the toothed whales, evolved as relatively small, fast flesh-eaters. In toothed whales, which pursued prey aggressively, a capacity to echolocate evolved. This was a trick of making high-frequency clicks with air compressed in sacs

40 Hz, cannot hear what they have to say. At 20 Hz, the vocalizations of finbacks are among the lowest-frequency sounds made by an animal on earth, and the sound waves of their communications travel underwater as far as fifteen miles. Fin whales become sexually mature between five and eleven years of age, females typically bearing one calf every three years—a slow, mammalian recruitment of young that betrays their origins as land animals. They bear their young for a full year, calving in December and January in the Northern Hemisphere; they nurse the calves, which at birth are twenty feet long and weigh two tons, for six to seven months.

Melville, in his infamous rant on "Cetology" in the thirty-second chapter of *Moby-Dick*, sees a timepiece in the finback whale's "grand distinguishing feature": "When the sea is moderately calm, and slightly marked with spherical ripples, and this gnomon-like fin stands up and casts shadows upon the wrinkled surface, it may well be supposed that the watery circle surrounding it somewhat resembles a dial, with its style and wavy hour-lines graved on it. On that Ahaz-dial the shadow often goes back."

Melville notes that the finback whale is the whale most commonly seen by boat passengers who, like me, have no particular business with them. With his characteristic blend of fact and fancy, he tries to turn the finback into an isolato:

> The Fin-Back is not gregarious. . . . Very shy; always going solitary; unexpectedly rising to the surface in the remotest and most sullen waters; his straight and single lofty jet rising like a tall misanthropic spear upon a barren plain; gifted with such wondrous velocity and power in swimming, as to

defy all present pursuit from man; this leviathan seems the banished and unconquerable Cain of his race, bearing for his mark that style upon his back.

Melville did not exaggerate the speed of the finback. A fin with business elsewhere or uncomfortable in the presence of a ship will be quickly gone, its size no hindrance to an impressive sprint. Five years after he departed from Jamestown for the last time, Captain John Smith sailed to the vicinity of Monhegan Island, fifty miles west of Mount Desert, with a "plot . . . to take Whales." An able fellow, Smith and his men were no match for the fin whales they encountered instead of the right whales they expected in the spring of 1614: "[W]e found this Whale-fishing a costly conclusion: we saw many, and spent much time in chasing them; but we could not kill any: They beeing a kinde of Jubartes, and not the Whale that yeeldes Finnes and Oyle as wee expected."

For a long time, in fact, fins were too fast to hunt. As right whales were being decimated from one side of the Atlantic to the other, these great finbacks, unprofitable to pursue, were largely left alone. The colonial author J. Hector St. John de Crèvecoeur, who incorrectly calls the cosmopolitan finback "an American whale," noted in 1782 that it was "never killed, as being too swift." Eventually technology caught up with that swiftness and, like other species of whales, the finback took its beating at the hands and harpoons of the whaling industry. Their populations were reduced worldwide until commercial whaling largely came to an end in 1971.

The Gulf of Maine is home to representatives of both suborders of whales, baleen and toothed whales. Among the former, the *Mysticeti*, are the familiar blue, finback, sei, minke, and humpback whales—all rorqual or tube whales—and the less frequently seen right, bowhead, and gray whales. Among the *Odontoceti* that might appear in the waters of the continental shelf off Mount Desert Island are beluga, sperm, and pilot whales, rarely killer whales and the bottlenose and beaked whales, as well as the smaller dolphins and porpoises.

To see any of these creatures, however briefly, is to confirm that the niche for Cetacea, perhaps the most ingenious order of mammals on the planet, is still being occupied in the gulf and is still part of the larger ecosystem of Mount Desert Island. Whales know the great counterclockwise gyre of the gulf and all its complex play of currents and upwellings from Cape Cod to Cape Sable, from Jeffreys Bank and Cashes Ledge to Georges Bank. They know the gulf in all its bathymetric complexity—its basins, shelves, shoals, and channels—and beyond the gulf, across Georges Bank, they know the Gulf Stream and what the ocean, the true ocean, feels like over the abyssal plains seventeen thousand feet below the surface of the sea.

As is true of many activities on Mount Desert, the feel of whale-watching is finer out of season. You see less but learn more. Searches tend to be slower and more thoughtful when the boat is not packed from rail to rail with a crowd eager to *ooh* and *aah* over a breaching humpback. Nothing wrong with that, and there are plenty of whales to see in summer—especially humpbacks and fins, often with young in tow, and pods of minke

in a whale's nasal passages. Sound waves could be directed in specific directions, the sonarlike echoes detected by ear bones suspended in fat, those echoes, in turn, triangulated by the convoluted brain of a hunting animal capable of turning on a dime toward a hint of prey. The mysticetes, the baleen whales, lost teeth in favor of mouths full of baleen. They grew to enormous size as filter feeders, taking great advantage of the quantity of passive prey adrift in the ocean's currents, the humble bottom of the planet's food chain. Buoyed by salt water and fed by the original fecundity of the ocean, they evolved to become not only the largest animals ever to live on this planet but among the most intelligent and well spoken.

When any whale surfaces, it brings into view the fifty million years of this evolutionary narrative, the story of a terrestrial vertebrate that went to sea. In whales, what is factual and what is mythopoetic about nature come greatly together. Melville knew that. No wonder we want to see them and that, when they surface or breach, it is so hard to perceive cetaceans for what they are. Whale-watching is easy. Seeing whales takes time.

Despite their exotic size, whales lead the same domestic lives all mammals lead. They feed and grow, mature and breed, using their quarter of the ocean, from the sub Arctic to the Caribbean, to survive as individuals and maintain viability as a population. They give birth and nurse and nurture and move through their years with what I imagine to be a kind of stoic calm as well as some awareness of sensual pleasure in their experiences, if only the neural-feedback loop that drives the will to live, the ambition to follow the seasons from the Caribbean to the sub-Arctic.

This is not to anthropomorphize: every living thing has some form of consciousness at the center of its experiences, every chordate has a brain lit with some form of mindfulness. Whales must sense in their central nervous system their power and grace, the force and flow of ocean currents, the variety of pressure and temperature in the grand waterscape through which they move. They must wonder in some fashion about the strange, bright expanse of the sky and have some relation we will never understand to unspeakable degrees of darkness and cold. They must experience some form of emotion when they detect the clicks, whistles, and keening of other whales. They must have some rudimentary sense of their fate as a kind, feel their numbers increasing or decreasing from year to year, have a communal awareness of what biologists call population.

That they must come to the surface of the sea to breathe is a tithe they pay as the cost of their primary evolutionary adaptation. That is when they were hunted and why we have a chance, trivial or profound, to watch them. We see whales at their most vulnerable moment, when their pelagic wildness is domesticated for just a few moments by that need to breathe—to fill lungs not much different, in principle, from ours—with the same oxygen that nourishes our blood.

Near the end of his fine book on the history of the Atlantic cod fishery, Mark Kurlansky derides whale-watching as one more sign of a decadent society, one that has done what Emerson warned us not to do—turn nature into a mere object for human amusement: "There is a big difference between living in a society that hunts whales and living in one that views them. Nature is being reduced to precious demonstrations for entertainment and education, something far less natural than hunting."

Kurlansky's point is well taken—hunting whales for sustenance was once a great tribal act, and the preindustrial hunting of whales was brave work indeed, as Crèvecoeur noted—but I wouldn't lump education with entertainment. In fact, education is the only tool we have left to save both whales and ourselves. Despite the tourist trappings of whale-watching—quite a carnival event on fair days in midsummer—being briefly in the presence of a whale can be the beginning and not the end of something. That finback is long gone from my view, as are all the whales I've seen. But their footprints still pond, blooming into the middle distance, on the surface of my consciousness any time I choose to remember. I'm not sure we can do much for whales, but that is what they do for us—they lead us on, shadowing us from below over the drowned peaks of the Inner Schoodic Ridge.

The romance of a whale sighting is undeniable and connects us with the fact and image of epic journeying. Whales organize the otherwise trackless colors of the sea, offer a living center in a foreground with an impossible horizon. They seem to point a *way*. For the ancients, the ocean was a "whale road," not an idle epithet. On overcast days, whales *are* the color of the sea. This is a trick of light, of course, but in both a factual and a metaphorical sense, whales are attributes of open water taken form, a climax expression of the ocean in the same way that bears embody the ecology and essence of a forest.

As Melville noted, a shadow cast by the dorsal fin of a cetacean on the surface of the sea is one way to mark time, one of nature's great revelations of life's originality and audaciousness. A whale gives meaning to open water in ways no other life form does. Whales, like pelagic birds, bring an aura of far-traveling to one point in space, carry great distances on their broad backs. Is there any finer image of departure on this planet than the thick tailstock of a humpback whale lifting that great animal's flukes for a terminal dive?

In the end, whales elude us, as Melville's Ishmael suggested they will always do. Pursue them with idle curiosity or meditative longing, they will not be had.

The reward for leaving Mount Desert Island is coming back, especially at sunset when the island is awash in changing light. Returning from whale-watching, I enjoy seeing from a distance the mountains where I walk and the coves and headlands I haunt from the perspective of someone coming to the island as it should be approached—from the sea. Tired of looking seaward at everything and nothing, you let the land reclaim your eyes and grow to fill your interests again. Fatigued with intently watching for one impossible thing—the body of the whale—let the landscape turn against the progress of the boat, let your eyes and mind rest on a nearer, more manageable horizon and less outlandish forms of life. Watch the outer islands and headlands grow and tack toward the boat, opening channels into the harbor as you approach.

Mount Desert assembles itself, turns and looms, hauntingly familiar. What Ishmael said about whales is true of islands—their "true form," their "absolute body" remains a mystery. With islands as with whales, things that live in water take on fluid shapes, the energy of one element tutoring the form of another. Perhaps that is why indigenous storytelling is so keen on metamorphosis and

why the Abenaki have so many myths that celebrate the cohabi-
tation of whalebacked mountains and mountainous whales in this
landscape.

Some evenings, coming toward Mount Desert, its mountains
glow like the long, sleek backs of fin whales surfacing through
the last light of day headed for Georges Bank and, beyond shoals
that once teemed with unimaginable fish life, toward the abyssal
plains of the true Atlantic, where even our imaginations cannot
follow them.

. . . *time often moves sideways* . . .

—JIM HARRISON,
"BURIED TIME"

MARSH TIME—

The Strong Presence of Things

Birds scatter with every paddle stroke.

Three killdeer flush, crying loudly, as I come into view in the lower marsh. Two spotted sandpipers careen off a nearby mud bank, peeping madly. A mature cormorant with two juveniles in tow slowly flaps off a rock. A hundred yards away, a great blue heron I hadn't seen unfolds itself from an edge of spartina grass and flies upmarsh, buoyed by deeply flexed wings, taking another heron with it fifty yards farther on.

Stir a salt marsh with a good ash paddle as carefully as you can and what birds you don't put to flight noisily you will send silently into the mesmerizing ranks of marsh grasses and dense thickets of heaths that offer you miles of shoreline without a useful place to put ashore. An inviting, ultimately impossible place, a salt marsh will fend you off as surely as it takes in what lives there. A marsh is, after all, another tidal zone, another venue where the edge of the sea works secretly in the open.

From early spring to autumn, I haunt Bass Harbor Marsh, a dendrite of brackish water that extends in two directions. One branch of it trends northwest toward the southern foot of Western Mountain. The other curls south toward the sphagnum bogs of Big Heath, reaching nearly all the way to the woods near Ship Harbor.

Sometimes after spending a day on open water watching whales and seabirds, I need the confines of the marsh to readjust my senses to a more manageable horizon, a chance to soak up a near view of things. I don't yet want the dense immediacy of a walk in the woods, but I need a day in the open yet close places of a marsh. I need flycatchers not shearwaters to contemplate, the slide of turtles rather than the breach of whales to catch my eye. After leaning against a ship rail for a day, the Gulf of Maine still seemed distant and would leave me needing the closer fit of a landscape I could reach out and touch—marsh grass and muck—but not walk into. So I'll kneel aft of center in my beamy twelve-foot Old Town canoe, balanced for the shallowest draft, and enjoy the comfortable feel of the marsh just off my shoulders. In the closest places, marsh grasses will hiss around the hull—sweet rustle of land's end in the offbeat wetland world—and I'll be eye level with the earth.

The lower reach of Bass Harbor Marsh, above Route 102, is an open, sometimes placid, sometimes wind-ruffled expanse of water. After years of paddling the marsh, I still haven't quite figured out the lag of high and low tides in its northern and southern branches, the offbeat way the marsh keeps time. Unlike the easily read rise and fall of seawater on the steep rock coast, tidal movement in a marsh is more difficult to read. Minutes and hours disappear into threading creeks, percolate in gray marsh mud. In a marsh—the farthest reach of the sea inland—the tide is horizontal. Time slips sideways, like light.

Past half-tide in either direction, water pours in and out of the marsh under the Route 102 bridge with authority. But high tide stays back in the creek heads well beyond the time posted for high tide at Bass Harbor Head, waits for hours sometimes in the spring when the upper wetlands are flooded with rainwater, before beginning to drop, slowly at first but eventually leaving that telltale muddy stain on the thick stems of marsh grasses. Those stems, like the tarred dock pilings in Bass Harbor, are as good a measuring stick as you will find for what the sun and the moon and the sea are up to. Low tide, too, takes forever to turn. The marsh waits, shrunk to its channels, mudflats exposed to gulls and other gleaners, last in line among coastal places to feel the Gulf of Maine push inland again.

After my first, ill-fated excursion years ago mucking around at low tide, my paddle blade heavy with dark gray mud, I learned to catch a rising tide and float easily into the marsh like a merganser. Any time you paddle tidal water, it's best to be headed—all cocky and smug—the way the water is going. Makes you look like you know what you're doing. The last two hours of a rising tide is ideal—an hour for slowly exploring the lower shoreline, watching the waterfowl of the open water and the hawk life of the open skies as the upper marsh slowly rises along the reedy roots of creekside grasses. Then an hour for paddling the winding upper reaches of Marshall Brook, which, if you proceed quietly, will dole out many rewards.

Marshall Brook proper disappears between Freeman and Clark Ridges, extending in two branches deep into hollows shadowed by the sharp southern ridges of Western Mountain. On the highest tides, you can paddle a bit past the mouth of Marshall Brook to a dead end below a small beaver dam that floods a wetland fed by a fan of small brooks.

Nose your canoe between those narrow banks. Listen to the spill of water, as pure a sound as you will ever hear, over and through the old dam. Watch warblers thread the sky over the wetland while woodpeckers cackle in the woods behind you. Be startled by the snort of a white-tailed deer somewhere in the shadows. Wonder about bear and moose. Note the tannic water level itself against stalks of cordgrass that seem, just when the marsh is perfectly full, to hold the ocean in their grip, water beading up their sandpapery stems.

For moments that are hard to measure, you'll think the ocean is going to stay up in the marsh forever. You will feel at a point of profound balance and be reluctant to move anything other than your eyes and ears. And when you finally stir a paddle again in the sky-whitened water before that untolled moment has passed, you'll have the sinking feeling that you have ruined that balance, inadvertently turned the tide with your own restlessness.

But that illusion, product of the mesmerizing quiet of the upper marsh, won't last long. A male northern harrier—a marsh hawk as gray as a great blue heron—will get up out of nowhere, flare skyward, and then get to hunting, hovering low over the marsh hay and leatherleaf. You can imagine the gouts of air percuss under its hammering wings and the fear in whatever hides beneath it quivering like the water starting to rill silently through the spartina.

Watch the water level carefully, and when that dark stain on the stems of the marsh grasses starts to lengthen, crank your boat around between the narrow banks and ride the outgoing tide as slowly as you can, nursing every inch of flow, every minute of falling water, timing your passage between widening shores to get yourself past the shallows near the mouth of Buttermilk Brook with enough water to float your shoe keel over the marsh mud with only a bump and drag or two to remind you of the quickening flow of the outgoing tide.

Some days you see nothing on the marsh except the way space is arranged—the open, prairie look of the salt-hay meadows, the changing silhouette of Western Mountain. On windy, overcast days, the choppy, gray water is unattractive and seems lifeless. Paddling is disappointing, a failure of engagement. The marsh seems to have no depth of field, offers no way for your mind to get a purchase on the foreground or the middle distance. Flat expanses fend you off. Birds hide or pass quickly overhead, looking for someplace better. And the gloom of the marsh in rain, when you paddle through a gusting mist, is as unsettling as it is unsatisfying.

Other days, especially when a high tide coincides with dawn or dusk, you will paddle through a quicksilver shimmer of blue water into an unearthly light, suddenly find yourself surrounded by what I can only call the sheer presence of things—what philosophers call *being-in-itself*—the life of the marsh not as an object of observation but as the self-contained subject of its own heartbeat and consciousness—a landscape worth regarding as carefully as we regard ourselves. On those mornings and evenings, that upper reach of Marshall Brook becomes a Möbius strip of syrupy water bulging elegantly with the gentle weight of the ocean leaning in, a ribbon of time folded into an impossible shape. Then Bass Harbor Marsh is one of the most beautiful places on earth, and only the coming of broad daylight or the darkness of evening will convince you that time—held somehow between the rustle of the marsh grasses and the call of unseen birds—is not standing perfectly and permanently still, offering you and everything around you a taste of immortality.

Set off for a few such timeless hours in mid-June, when the marsh is tense with nesting and predation. Flush the ever-present cormorants off their rock and watch the herring gulls commuting over the lower marsh. Listen to song sparrows and red-winged blackbirds in the bankside vegetation, male black-capped chickadees in the nearby woods. Enjoy that open, western look of the lower marsh, the broad expanses of salt-hay meadow threaded with hidden creeks. Listen for the rare *glunk* of bitterns or the cries of snipe. Breathe in the warm, rich marsh funk. From the wide water admire the indigenous profile of Western Mountain, that long, well-sculpted ridge that oversees the western half of Mount Desert Island. You paddle toward Little Notch and then a little more to the west toward Great Notch, both quiet, deep-woods trail crossings well worth frequenting.

An osprey or two will school your awareness of the sky, maybe a broad-winged hawk will trace the treeline, or a male northern harrier will wheel stiffly over a distant stretch of marsh. Occasionally a loon will appear and then disappear, this shapely bird the platonic form of an avian sleekness more suited to swimming than flying. Male mallards in groups of twos or threes fly hard toward Bass Harbor, where they may condescend to grub around the docks. Black ducks keep close quarters, staying in the shadows of the marsh edge, hoping not to be noticed.

When you run out of broad water, you turn a bit west of north, guided by the curves of an emerald-green shoreline and by a hint of deeper, darker, less ruffled water in what passes for the channel of Marshall Brook. From here you can see the fire tower on Beech Mountain, where you watch the hawk migration in the fall, and you can see the glacial notch that you know is occupied by Long Pond, where you troll streamers for landlocked salmon in spring.

Somehow the effect of the marsh narrowing is a loss of sky. In these closer quarters, enjoy the way you can rudder the landscape around with a deft brace of your paddle, swing the marsh quickly this way and that with short sweeps and draws as you try to keep good water under your hull. The small sounds the canoe makes in the water, the slurry of the paddle and the boat's modest wake all seem scaled to the peaceful ways of the marsh. There is a purity to paddling a marsh where you need no more boat skill than a floating leaf and where your presence does not disturb the raspy, insistent three-note call of the alder flycatchers in the shoreline vegetation or the hermit thrush hidden out of sight deeper in the woods.

The marsh will refine all your senses. Watch for the movement of disappearance in the nearby grasses, the hints of game trails that wind down to the water's edge, the ripples and flashes of fish and turtles. Watch the drooping seed heads of the grasses themselves. The slowly closing banks direct your eye to hummocks of heaths and stands of spruce, spindly tamarack standing incongruously here and there as the marsh rises toward higher ground. Admire the sentinels of weathered spruce snags that picket the upper marsh and the dense, living woods behind them. Try to see heron, gray as the snags, before they see you. Trace the swooping flight of a kingfisher in your mind, memorizing its shallow arc trailing behind the noisy bird's cocky profile. Enjoy how common eagles are. Admire crows.

The marsh dares you to get close to all these things, to become one with its otherness, to pay attention, to learn, to be satisfied, as marsh life is, with its own unnamable being. One time up Marshall Brook I noted a distinctive squeaky wheel call that broke down into chirps. I enjoyed this persistent vocalization up and down the brook, but could not get the birds in my binoculars. A warbler I didn't know. Days later, on the deck of my cabin, I realized these chirping, squeaking wheels were Nashville warblers, something a better birder would have known instantly. I was glad to have figured out the species but enjoyed remembering when all I could do was listen to them call and wonder what they were.

The art of being on a marsh is the art of witnessing. The silhouettes of a least flycatcher, the singing of a solitary vireo, the sudden swoop of a pileated woodpecker across the water in front of you, or a furtive shift of sparrows or winter wrens. They all have something to reveal about themselves, about the evolution of life, and—when you strive to pay attention to them—about the quality of your own awareness of the world. Marshes are generous in the way they dole out their distractions and then credit us with the attentiveness of seeing and hearing, of coming to know or at least to recognize, to ask at almost every turn, *What was that?* The marsh dares us to come know it consciously, but it also tutors us in being satisfied with an unconscious, purely sensory awareness of the extraordinary weave of life it harbors.

If the marsh doesn't startle you with a frank offering—like a burst of wood ducks as you come quietly around a bend—it will give gifts with the same offbeat rhythm as it sifts the tide through its muddy creeks, instantly reveal to you something you did not know, or offer you the chance of a delayed epiphany.

Late one spring, the lower marsh hissed at me—a sound I had never heard before. *A rattling hiss*, I noted in my journal, *like small castanets*. I was paddling the shoreline to see what I could see, before heading up the south branch at flood tide, hoping to have enough water to make the woods beyond the marsh.

Before the shoreline marsh grasses started hissing at me, my notes were confidently full of the names of things—goldfinches, cormorants, a male northern harrier, crows, red-winged black-birds, herring gulls, a pair of mallards. These birds were more than their names, of course. I noted that the harrier was *gray as a heron, with black-tipped wings, yellow legs and, even from a distance, what are clearly prodigious talons*, and that the male mallard's green neck looked blue from certain angles. I noted that cormorants taking off from some low rocks slapped their tails on the water until they got airborne.

The heart of my notes is about what I did not know, the source of the hissing, a minor mystery. But the purpose of experience is, in part, to take us from one local unknown to another, expanding and revising our awareness of things. The advantage of being a self-taught naturalist is that I am slow to recognize what I do not know and can enjoy the process of stumbling through the act, the art of recognition. When you are untutored, everything is *diagnostic*, to borrow a useful term from field guides I carry with me. The drone of expertise informs but does not teach. I can, at times, rattle off lists of what I do know as tediously as anyone with an appetite for identification. But out exploring the recesses of Mount Desert Island, or in nature anywhere, I am always pleased to encounter what I cannot name, to find experience for which I do not yet have language. So I paddled back and forth for a half hour along that gently, oddly hissing shoreline, staring into the grasses until I needed to get upmarsh on that flood tide.

I came back out a few hours later, carrying more names and notes with me—*the fine silhouette of a kingfisher in flight, monochrome against the too-bright sky*; the sight of crows successfully harassing a bald eagle, a mismatch I did not understand; the familiar calls of towhees and white-throated sparrows in the woods as well as the ever-present black-throated green warblers in the canopy and hermit thrushes on the ground.

I noted, as I always did, odd details about the way the tide turns in the upper marsh, a blend of fact and impressions that might help me judge high water more accurately. I spent a complicated hour sneaking up on a broad-winged hawk in a spruce snag, approaching it by degrees along the bends of the winding brook. At the farthest reach of my paddling, I heard a snort that sounded as if it had the great black nose of a moose behind it, rather than the delicate muzzle of a white-tailed deer, but that might have been wishful thinking.

And then, coming back out into the lower marsh, the hissing again, which I had forgotten about.

Now any competent birder would have known all along that

this hissing was the call of sharp-tailed sparrows on their nests in hummocks of black grass, which rose here and there among the *Spartina patens.* Once I heard the hissing again, I quietly waited alongshore for the bird to show itself in the early evening light. I knew I was waiting well when two black ducks, a wary species, swam by within ten feet of me.

Turns out, I wrote—stopping for an unusually discursive burst of note-taking in the canoe, I was so involved in this field moment—*to be a beautiful little sparrow, very small like a Savannah; suddenly see it on the edge of a blade of marsh grass, some color in its face and a delicate sharp tail; this is the hissing bird; olive in its face and head and back of neck; think maybe for a moment it is a flycatcher but no it is sparrow-like, clearly a sparrow: brown back, white throat, big dark eye, and olive or yellow in the face; call a hissing with a chip chip. This is the gift of the day, this marsh sparrow*: hiss chip chip.

This is how I like to learn the names of things. Every kind of habitat, like a salt marsh, has a way of doling out such experiences. In the end, I suppose it must all come down to language for a writer. But it needs to begin, as Emerson suggested, with direct experience—with sensation and the freedom of not knowing and the pleasure of coming to know or to understand something that you did not understand before. Learning the names of things is part of that—especially for those of us who enjoy the poetry in the Latin binomials of Linnaean classification—and it puts one not at the end of knowing but at the threshold of the natural history and evolution of another living being. Armed with a name, one can learn much from books. But the character of one's first experience of a species is determined by the quality of an unschooled encounter. The hissing, chipping sharp-tailed sparrow in the marsh turns out to be the saltmarsh sharp-tailed sparrow. Sometimes names lead us to a comic redundancy, a paddling through the mirror of words and things.

The marsh invites you to join its balance, to purify your intentions, to first become a respectful observer and then to try to observe from the perspective of what you observe, not only to notice and finally name in your mind the sharp-tailed sparrow hiding in the marsh grasses but to try to look out at the marsh through the sparrow's eye, to enjoy the ratio of what you know about the world around you and what you don't know, to feel as keenly as a hawk the innocence of the marsh and the potential purity of one's presence there as you try to observe without disturbing, try to be there without being there, like a heron frozen in a wooden posture. There is no place in a salt marsh for an acquisitive biped with a heavy tread, literally nowhere to stand. The marsh also invites you to perceive the order of its ecology, the narrative of its natural life. Of all places I spend time on Mount Desert, my field notes and journals from marsh paddling seem the most composed.

In the end, a marsh is best measured by its breadth rather than its depth, and perhaps even better by the intricacies of its constantly changing shape. Marshes sharpen the eye and mind, schooling attention with a demanding foreground. Marsh inhabitants school the ear to pay attention and direct movement, tutor a subtle synesthesia—the call of a cuckoo puts you in mind of a sleek shape and curved bill; the call of a broad-wing brings the authority of stiff-winged raptor flight to mind. Marshes train the eye to perceive subtle motions, blends of color, tricks of vegetative form that simultaneously conceal and reveal the life within.

And, of course, a salt marsh is the final expression of the marine world, the idea of the sea come quietly to the edge of meadows and woods, the fringe of ocean become a woodland thing.

At high tide, a marsh may be the quietest place on earth, tense with its own fullness, which, like the turn of the tide elsewhere, occurs during some unnoticeable moment. On a marsh you sense, better than anywhere else, that time is neither created nor destroyed, and that despite the artificial movement of our clocks and the natural movement of the tide, that time, in passing, does not move, that each moment is perfectly still. Some mornings and some evenings, the subtle play of tide and light in the upper reaches of Bass Harbor Marsh redeems time in this way, makes of all time one still moment.

. . . the ghosts of glaciers drift
among those folds and folds of fir . . .

—ELIZABETH BISHOP,
"CAPE BRETON"

RIVER OF MOUNTAINS—

Naming Names

The deep waters of Somes Sound divide Mount Desert Island roughly in half, its length running parallel to the trend of the famous eastern summits, all of which have long southern ridges that taper down to the sea. The depths of the sound, like the depths of Mount Desert's glacial lakes, are another elegant trace of the southward advance and northward retreat of the glaciers that gouged, plucked, and filed the coast of Maine. The basins of the sound and the lakes are mirror images of the mountains that throw shadows across them. Rocky heights juxtaposed to watery depths are fundamental to the dynamic balance, the casual poise of great forces in apparent arrest that gets into your soul on Mount Desert Island. Walking in this landscape, you sometimes feel that some great event had just settled into place.

The bulk of the eastern half of the island is built of what has come to be called the granite of Cadillac Mountain, the pink bedrock everyone who loves Mount Desert Island can see in their sleep. That monumental pink rock drew nineteenth-century painters to the island, and when they reproduced its distinctive hue in their landscapes, art critics in New York chided their lack of realism. But the color of the rock is real enough, and the ignorance of critics a passing thing.

West of Somes Sound, Cadillac granite is less dominant and persists only as a mile-wide band of bedrock carved into the modest peaks and steep ridges that oversee the western half of the island. North and south of that band lies a puzzle of other bedrock, evidence of the great forces and changes that buckled the island into its rugged shape. South of Western Mountain lies a band of the dark, big-boulder shatter zone that sheaths the tips of the eastern peninsulas, the brooding tidal-zone rock of Little Hunters Beach, where I like to watch storms come in.

Other Devonian granites come into play on the western half of the island, the granites of Somesville to the north and Southwest Harbor to the south. There are beds of volcanic tuffs apparently solidified out of ash falls from the volcanic activity that did some of the terra-forming here and on the outer islands. There is a scattering of other granite, most notably on the southwest tip of the island on either side of Ship Harbor and at Seawall and around Pretty Marsh Harbor. And in places along the western margin of Mount Desert you find bands of Ellsworth Schist, the oldest bedrock here.

Historical names overlay the geologic. Acadia and St. Sauveur Mountains, Valley Peak, and Flying Mountain flank a gentle curve in the southwest shoreline of Somes Sound, where you can anchor safely in the lee of just about any bad weather and, in spring and summer, hear the cries of the peregrine falcons that nest above Valley Cove. To the west, Beech Cliff, Canada Cliff, and Beech Mountain rise to flinty exposures of bare rock between the glacial gouges filled by Echo Lake and Long Pond, the southern end of which is as dark and mountain-haunted a body of water on gloomy days as is Somes Sound. Beyond Long Pond, Western Mountain—a distinctively notched, double-peaked ridge—arcs toward Seal Cove Pond, once a saltwater embayment by the look of it on a topographic map. It now drains through an elegant crease of that shatter-zone rock into Seal Cove and the Eastern Passage to Blue Hill Bay.

The modest mountains of what has come to be called the "Quietside" of Mount Desert Island—peaks much less monumental and celebrated than Champlain, Cadillac, Penobscot, and Sargent—play out the theme of a rugged coastal island in a minor key, the music of which rises and falls as abruptly as their steep slopes. Walk these western trails and you will see things—moments in the lives of birds and animals, shifts in weather and light, the changing look of dark woods, and unexpected vistas. You need to know these western peaks and valleys and their woods to know Mount Desert.

Get out early, walking through the woods just after dawn so that you can enjoy morning light from the rough exposures on Acadia Mountain overlooking Somes Sound, or from the smooth, tan rocks of Beech Mountain, or from that slanting granite bald on the eastern side of Mansell Mountain, from which you get a fine view of Southwest Harbor. Westward, these craggy, well-forested highlands descend onto the broad ledges of rock that staircase down the western edge of Western Mountain toward Seal Cove Pond, a fine place to sit and watch the sunset, looking out toward Bartlett Narrows and, beyond, the still fields and dark forests of Bartlett Island—that idyllic place—toward Blue Hill Bay and the puzzle of hills, inlets, and farther islands of the Penobscot Bay horizon.

Most of this unassuming backcountry is protected within the confines of Acadia National Park, a blessing that grows in importance as more and more of the island succumbs to the inevitable development of a popular place in an overpopulated world. But even before the establishment of the park in 1919 (as Lafayette National Park), these quiet places on the western side of the island were popular with walkers. There were paths, trails, and primitive roads on Western Mountain and in the Beech Mountain area from at least the 1870s and likely long before that. And most of the paths we walk now on the Quietside—on Acadia Mountain, St. Sauveur, Valley Peak, and Flying Mountain—show up, well established, on maps published just after the end of the Civil War. Mount Desert Island has had a rich history of trails and recreational walking and is, in fact, a living museum of trail-making and trail-marking techniques and fashions over the last century and a half. You are always walking in someone else's footsteps here, hoping to encounter an original moment on an old path. Some of the cairns that guide your way are older than mossy stumps.

Looking over old maps, you find old names, apt descriptors or casually wrought local names or traces of nearly forgotten incidents, reminding you that before it became a famous tourist destination and a watering hole for the infamous "rusticators,"

Mount Desert Island was simply a rural place. Busy with industry—fishing, quarrying, logging, farming—but rural with the communal humor and wit of local life.

After the national park was formed,* there was a tendency to monumentalize a landscape that needed no embellishment. Human vanity leads to naming natural places after human beings, often following a suspect "great man" theory of history. So, on the eastern half of the island, Newport Mountain became Champlain Mountain, Dry Mountain became Dorr Mountain, Green Mountain became Cadillac. I admire Samuel de Champlain, one of the most intelligent discoverers of his time. And I admire George B. Dorr, justly known as the "father of Acadia National Park." But I don't need their names attached to mountains, which have lives of their own.

I keep it as an article of faith that no human being deserves to have a mountain named after him (or her). What, if you love the being of mountains, could be more tasteless? I prefer either natural names for natural places or whatever can be rescued of indigenous names, though neither the Passamaquoddy nor the Penobscot seem to have had an appetite for anything more than pragmatic designations. Their likely carry-trails across the island—canoe portages that linked waterways from the inland to the seaward side—were thought to have been unmarked and unimproved. Preindustrial peoples, occupied with survival, did not advertise or promote, and they had, given a keener awareness of their dependence on nature, an earthier sense of the relation between words and things.

---

* Lafayette National Park was renamed Acadia National Park in 1929.

We are fortunate that Champlain, struck by the sheer fact of this island, named it not for some king or princeling but for how it looked to him from the sea. *Pemetic*—the Passamaquoddy name for the island would do nicely; *Mount Desert* is not bad. Restoring some of the place names of the fine, sepia-toned topographic map published in Edward Rand's *Flora of Mount Desert Island* in 1894 strikes me as a way to ease language back into synch with nature and the more important history here, the history of the lives of ordinary people.

Naming is a hit-or-miss art. The earliest known European naming here bears an almost indigenous sense of a designation so simple and apt that it is reverential even though, ironically, it is inaccurate. Somes Sound appears as *Rio de Montañas* on Diego Ribero's 1529 world map. Although a misnomer based on Estevan Gomes's incomplete reconnaissance of the sound in 1525, the name captures perfectly the look and feel of Somes as you sail or paddle into it through the narrows at its mouth, feeling deep water under your keel and the dark shelter of steep cliffs all around you. *River of Mountains* covers the case. And the appellation inadvertently suggests something important about the poetics of a landscape where the mountains as well as the rivers seem to flow. No disrespect to the Englishman Abraham Somes, who founded the island's first town, Somesville, in 1761, but in the absence of an Abenaki name for the great body of water that divides Mount Desert Island in half, *Rio de Montañas* would do nicely.

I suppose there's nothing wrong with the more recent names, except that some of them displaced the ways Mount Desert Islanders had come to refer to their landscape by the end of the nineteenth century, just before the "summer people" started to move onto the island in force and the frenetic jollity of tourism took over the island for nearly half the year. But it's unlikely there would ever be agreement on which old names should be revived. I rather like the name Acadia Mountain, harking back as it does to the original, lyrical French designation—*l'Acadie*—for their claims on the North American coast between the 40th and 46th parallels. According to Samuel Eliot Morison, the French was an approximation of an indigenous word for "The Place," one of those phatic designations frequently attributed, correctly or incorrectly, to Native Americans. But Acadia Mountain was once Robinson Mountain, if only because a Robinson once owned it, and was undoubtedly called something else before that. St. Sauveur, which commemorates an early, ill-fated Jesuit colony, might just as well become Dog Mountain, for whatever obscure reason that appellation satisfied the people who called it that.

Many current descriptive names have deep roots, and it's good to know, glancing at the old maps, that they have long been useful—Valley Peak, Flying Mountain, Valley Cove, Beech Cliff, Beech Mountain, and Canada Cliff. But what used to be simply the east and west peaks of Western Mountain became Mansell and Bernard Mountains after great men—more proper naming than this unassuming ridge needs.

Under any names, these Quietside trails reward walking. On good days, the landscape becomes nameless again—perhaps the goal of all walking here—a bunched fold of forested rock hills separated by deep lakes and ponds and arms of the sea. Disappear on a June morning into the tangled loops of paths between Echo

Lake and Somes Sound. Start toward Acadia Mountain as early as you can get out, the bulk of your breakfast still in your pack. Enjoy the calls of black-throated green warblers in the dark, spruce-fir woods and the way, if it has been a wet spring, the static of traffic on Route 102 is replaced by the liquid rustle of Man o' War Brook, a rill of clear water barely visible in the leaf litter that collected in its bed last winter. Scramble up a steep pitch of wet, jagged rock, bending to the angle of a cliff that, when you are feeling fit, seems not to resist you but to lift you up. In the morning, anyway, these short, steep pulls can feel like that. Get quickly eye level with a canopy that is full of the rattling of yellow-rumped warblers and maybe some nuthatches *peenting* in the woods below.

The first outcrop offers a view west of Echo Lake. The echoes from here are visual, the first suggestion of the theme that will be repeated all day—that the lay of the land is everything, that the shape of land and water here have profound causes, and that what grows or lives here is wise with natural wisdom. People have been walking here for two centuries simply because they want to move through this landscape, be a part of it, belong to it. The trail threads west through rock and pitch pine.

A little farther on, you get a view of the mouth of Somes Sound, a few miles off, see that the tide is up but falling and that a low-lying fog hangs around Greening Island. The next pull brings the mainland into view to the north and east, with Somes Sound growing into its full length below you. To the west, Beech Mountain rises into view and you get the idea of how the island's foremost bedrock plays itself out toward Blue Hill Bay. If you trudge along too quickly, you will miss the theory and practice of walking here, the way these paths ask you to stop at every turn and rise, to breathe deep and look and listen, to take in, through your boots and brains, where you are.

From the summit of Acadia, where that breakfast comes in handy, the landscape invites you to contemplate the River of Mountains below you and the expansive view of Mount Desert Island in all directions, not so much the names but the shapes of things, those ratios of land, water, and sky that will either grab you deeply or send you back down the trail in search of other entertainments.

There is, after the modest effort of getting to the center of Mount Desert Island, the heart of *l'Acadie* as one might now think of it, nothing else to do. The contemplation invited here is visceral not intellectual, and a little physical fatigue helps settle one down to the task. How can I be a healthy animal here—I think that is the question this landscape begs we ask. How can I become native to this place?

Somehow observation is a difficult art—not because we do not know the names of things but because we are estranged from our senses, from our instinctual, animal awareness of what and where we are. It has taken twenty years for my note-taking in the field to begin to become useful to me in the study.

Think I hear a hermit thrush, or some thrush below in the woods. Many of them. Hear the yellow rumps, sometimes a nuthatch, hum of boat motors, wind in my ears. Not much else. You can hear yourself think but your thoughts are immediately pruned back, like the pine. What's to say? Even the names of things seem shorn away. Just the sea breeze and the rocky puzzle pieces of the outer islands.

And this from my journal after staying for an hour on the summit of Acadia on June 2, 2005:

Two great black-backed gulls coming up on a thermal, spiraling slowly. Fine birds to see up close this way, in flight. Tail feathers translucent. You wait, you get into this landscape, something comes to you.

The pine, these pitch pine, becomes strong company.

Small waxy, oblong-leaved, rock-hugging plant coming into flower. Five-petalled white flowers, ½". Other things growing in the frost cracks of the granite.

Fishing boat working a purse seine in the middle of the Sound, in the lower end, running circles all morning. Catching what? Herring maybe, bait for lobster traps.

Glassing for peregrines in front of Valley Cove.

Crows. Common as the pitch pine, but a strong presence also.

Even herring gulls look distinguished when they are out on their own, framed as individuals against the summit air.

Large raptor, osprey or eagle-size in immature coloring— brown, dark leading edges of wings, white body underneath and white v on chest, dark elsewhere underneath, broad unmarked tail. Head white with black markings (like osprey). Immature osprey?

And so it goes. In the end, I would make no further claim than these frank notations of things seen—named or unnamed—of life doing what it does when left to its instincts and inclinations— raptor and rock, flower and tree—in a quiet, unspoiled place.

The walk down the steep southeastern side of Acadia is as fine as the stiff walk up the western side. You descend toward Somes Sound, good company from these highlands on its western shore, toward the mouth of Man o' War Brook, which has long been out of sight and hearing, having taken a direct route to the shore. Unless you are intent on trudging along watching your boot tops, you will stop to lean on your hiking stick every thirty yards or so as your descent turns you this way and that.

On the last high vantage before the trail descends back into the woods, I stop to glass the cliffs of Valley Peak and the blue air above Valley Cove for the peregrine falcons that nest there every year. I'm too far away to hear their cries, but I know from experience that peregrines would appear as pure motion, the air gathered into a slim-winged, blue-gray form hovering with much more agility than a broad-winged *Buteo* such as a red-tailed hawk or northern harrier, and with more predatory acumen in its slender shape than even bald eagles or osprey carry in their larger forms.

If you have ever seen a peregrine stoop, folded into the most aerodynamic animal shape on earth, moving faster than any animal on earth travels, you look for that potential holding in the sky, that beautiful lethality hovering in its hair-trigger way between those pointed wingtips while eyes that may be the platonic form of all seeing consider the space below it.

And if you have seen peregrines up close, as I have at hack sites—where captive-reared birds are released to the wild—you know what to look for when you search them out at a distance. Watch for the slender, blue-gray bird soaring on the warm air the morning sun sends up the cliff face or stooping on some doomed butterfly or passerine. Coming down the trail from Acadia

Mountain in spring and summer, I often see them. And, if not, watching for them—bringing an expectation of peregrines to the mountain—is a useful practice.

On that early June day in 2005, I did not see peregrines at that last vantage, though I watched for a good long time. But when I turned to go, I found myself confronting a pitch pine, not ten feet from me, full of cedar waxwings, a strange study in form and color. I'd never seen this ethereal, painterly bird up close and had never seen it in this most painterly of trees.

The pitch pine, as I've noted, is a wild expression of vegetative tenacity, especially where it is harshly pruned on Mount Desert's bare summits. Twisted into any form, this common, scaly barked tree is beautiful, a study in how satisfying form arises from irregularity and asymmetry. In the mountains, no two pitch pines are alike. Cedar waxwings, all identical, are common also, though uncommon in appearance and a kind of visual contradiction. In some ways the species looks delicate, ornate, and tropical— crested and masked, secondaries tipped a waxy red, tails banded a glossy yellow—but in other ways these tan-and-gray birds seem hardy, utilitarian, and boreal—like jays. Fill a pitch pine with waxwings—like the scene I confronted—and you have a moment to marvel at and puzzle over the artifice of nature, the complicated guises it takes.

In the end, the sheer particularity of their presence is what mattered—two forms of life on display, juxtaposed for no reason but to striking effect, and offering a lesson on looking and seeing.

Turn around, perhaps the message was, *don't fixate on what is not there. Look behind you.*

That's what you find in Acadia, a stop-time moment or two during a long, pleasant day of walking—moments not of what in religion and literature is sometimes called epiphany, but moments when you have transcended needing any revelation beyond the well-composed experience of a well-drawn present moment. This time, a field moment did not arise from the peregrine falcons I came to see but coalesced around the unexpected appearance of cedar waxwings in a pitch pine, birds I could almost reach out and touch, although for that one long moment the tree, alive with the colorful sheen of these monkish birds, looked as unreal as anything in a dream.

If I were more formally reverential, I would have made a shrine there, a small cairn to mark the spot like a T'ang dynasty poet. But it's best to resist pretension on the trail. I'm just a walker. The birds departed one by one, the tree reassumed its birdless self, and I moved on.

In Mount Desert's quiet places you walk from field moment to field moment until you understand the eventfulness of every step you take, see the fullness in the spaces between the mountains, come to know the island as a way of carefully spending time, as a school for tutoring and focusing your awareness, a place suggestive at every turn of a way of being.

Late one September, I came back to the peregrines at Valley Cove. I was taking an early autumn walk on the Ledge Trail and the St. Sauveur Mountain Trail south to Valley Peak and then down to Fernald Cove. For most of the trek I was content just to absorb the color and vivacity of the autumn woods, the bracing coolness in the air.

I took the Flying Mountain Trail back north along the shore of Somes Sound. This trail is closed in spring and part of summer while the peregrines nest, a necessary concession to their need for an undisturbed place. The trail takes you up over Flying Mountain, from which you have a low, wide-angle view of The Narrows, of the way Greening Island divides the entrance to the sound, and the enviable situations of Southwest and Northeast Harbors—both still perfect coastal towns of their kind.

The trail then led me down to Valley Cove, where I dawdled a bit watching loons and gulls on the ruffled water of a windy autumn day and enjoyed the weighty look of Somes Sound from eye level. I watched a bald eagle flying west over Flying Mountain and an osprey working the air over the cove. The steep cliffs of Valley Peak show as one of the densest thatches of contour lines on the Mount Desert Island topographic map. The base of those cliffs has weathered into the same kind of boulder-size scree you find on the slopes to the west of Jordan Pond and Long Pond, a slow recycling of frost-shattered granite.

The trail slabs up across the lower end of that scree, and while I scrambled up through it, I could hear what I knew were the cries of peregrines above me. At first I confused them with the osprey that was now flying back and forth close to the cliff face. Their calls may well have been some territorial complaint. I noted and still remember the osprey slashing the air maybe a hundred feet out, just visible through the trees, and the cries of the peregrines above us both. By the time I moved into the shadow of some ancient white birch—the third gift of this walk—I was winded but rich with a juxtaposition of focal points.

Although I was glad to cross paths with at least the cries of the peregrines and to observe the osprey's claims and the stocky power of its flight, those big old white birch seemed, when I got under the welcome shade of their influence, to anchor the moment. Noble with age, double- and triple-trunked regrowth from some rough wind-pruning perhaps, they were as strange as trees in *Lord of the Rings*, halfway to being Ents and fully up to holding court with the cries of peregrines and the belligerent flight of an osprey.

That was a long day traversing familiar ground in a new season, walking well-trod paths that never seem to lose their originality. I gave myself over to the pleasant fatigue that works on you in this rocky, uneven place where you are almost always ascending or descending. Toward the end of a good long day, the landscape may seem to walk through you as Zen teachings suggest will happen when contentment and fatigue join forces. You get Mount Desert in your head sometimes. The rough shoulders and quiet ravines of those mountains on the west shore of Somes Sound walked through me down the Flying Mountain Trail that day, and walked through me up that steep pitch on St. Sauveur that winds me every time. Dog Mountain, indeed. Dog-tired it leaves me, forcing me to stop and look around long after I have burned up the energy to be observant.

When I stopped, heart and lungs defeated a bit by the climb, I saw the peregrines, silent, wheeling below me, the osprey no longer in sight. I'd come right up through their world, the space of their lives, no more welcome than the osprey and only the faintest kin to anything here. And now I was moving on and they had released themselves to the air. All walks cohere as natural narrative. Breathing easier, I was satisfied to understand that this one had, finally, cohered around the lives of peregrine falcons, and of an osprey, and of those ancient white birch. I was rich to have seen them.

Peripherally the ocean
marks itself
against the gauging land

—A. R. AMMONS,
"EXPRESSIONS OF SEA LEVEL"

PARALLAX—

Expressions of Sea Level

In a kayak, you can feel two kinds of vertigo at sea level.

There is the mesmerizing stillness of placid water at dawn and dusk—a pink or blue hour laced with loons calling and ducks hurtling overhead, the chug of lobster boats trailing fat wakes that, overwhelmed by distance, never reach you. These are moments when time rarifies into a kind of visual music and you feel a frank sympathy with everything you observe. You sit in the water with no more self-consciousness than an eider. In this still hour, the totemic face of a harbor seal staring at you from twenty feet away is not the object of your contemplation but a subject keenly contemplating you.

You can become dizzy with this glassy stillness when the waters of Frenchman Bay or Pretty Marsh Harbor or Mount

Desert Narrows, which separates Mount Desert Island from the mainland, seem as depthless as the water in a painting. You may, at times, glassing scoters at a distance or staring into the near water watching great urns of knotweed standing at high tide, forget you are in a kayak and, turning, suddenly feel the craft squirrel around under you. And sometimes, when a cove is perfectly still, bathed in the pure, transient light of morning or evening, you can feel your boat, agitated only by your breathing, lose its purchase on the water. You can capsize in this stillness.

Or you might be lost in watching black guillemots bring food to their nests in the crannies of cliffs on Burnt Porcupine Island. They fly into and out of the shadows like bees working a hive. There's nothing to see, really, but you can't stop watching them through binoculars. Just the fact of small alcids tending their young on weathered exposures is enough to take you out of yourself. If you understand the poignancy of seabirds nesting on shelves of bare rock, you will watch them until you forget, paddle draped across your lap, that you are floating in Frenchman Bay.

And then there are moments of vertigo in rough water when you feel not so much the depth but the breadth of the ocean grab the chine of your hull, when you feel, even in inland waters, the authority of tide and wind, the weight of millions of gallons of water flowing with a purpose that can be unsettling and the uncanny force of a long fetch of wind that can be unforgiving.

When salt water moves out to sea—especially when it snakes deeply between steep-sided islands with a pronounced height of tide—the proximity of land means nothing. You concentrate on the water immediately around you, paddling squarely into the waves coming at you and riding the swells rolling under you. You keep your shoulders square to the horizon and your hips synched to the way your kayak is trying to track through the water, give in to the tumult around you while holding a firm line. You trust your boat, even when you can't see your bow. In difficult water, you paddle the fine line between concern and exhilaration and keep your mind on where you are going.

I've gotten in a rough play of tide and wind a few times in the waters around Mount Desert Island, always when the wind blew harder than predicted or shifted around to an unexpected quarter. If you are prepared to deal with changing conditions, it's good water to learn on—especially if you like to count coup from island to island the way I do, keeping a lee shore within reach.

From shore, coastal waters look like a simple expanse of blue or gray, and the tide seems to move innocently up and down, in and out. From a distance, the height and the period of waves seem unimportant. In a kayak as in a sailboat, you need a keener consciousness and more language for the constantly changing business of tidal waters—for the tricks of wind and the shifting character of tidal sets, as well as for the shape and behavior of waves.

One October I watched a fair day go bad from Dogfish Cove on the south side of Bartlett Island. A modest southwest wind that's usually helpful to paddlers stiffened while I had lunch, poked around all the lion's mane jellyfish stranded on the cobble beach, and birded the shoreline for warblers, kinglets mostly, zipping between the spruce tops.

As I lingered on shore, the wind picked up. Strong gusts started whitening the waters of the cove. Before I knew it, a pronounced sea was running, piling thick waves onto the beach. My safe, pleasant harbor was becoming a trap. There is about a five-mile fetch of open water, just past the northwest end of Hardwood Island, to Brooklin peninsula, and that stiff southwest wind was working up the open water and sending endless ranks of steep waves at the south shore of Bartlett Island and, beyond that, into Bartlett Narrows. Watching this mess, my stomach tightened, and I knew I would have a chore just getting back around Eastern Point into the relative shelter of the Narrows.

Psychologically tempting as it would be to hug the shoreline of Bartlett Island for the false comfort of having land nearby, the unfriendly mess of waves near shore—a product of that contending wind and tide—reminded me that on coastal waters the safest distance between two points is rarely a straight line. With a minimum of turning in those steep waves and deep troughs, I needed to get that wind behind me, where it would push me into the mouth of the Narrows.

This would be something new—a little advanced work for an intermediate paddler. I knew that when conditions suddenly change, the main thing is to think through what you need to do and then execute your plan methodically, my plan being a triangulation of Eastern Point—the near entrance to the Narrows—that would keep me out of beam seas for all but a turn at the apex of the triangle. That turn would leave me headed back up into the Narrows with the wind at my back. A strong falling tide would be flowing against me, and I assumed that would make for a few hundred yards of hard chop as the forces of wind and tide banged against each other.

I stowed everything but my paddle float and a water bottle in the hatch, fitted the skirt down tight, cinched my vest, strung the paddle lash, and, with zero freeboard, chugged out through Dogfish Cove into the wind. I took a fixed measure of concern, my planned course and that pit in my stomach with me, but they were all properly stowed too. I remember enjoying, in a grim way, slashing head-on into those four-foot seas, feeling—and trusting—the corky buoyancy of the kayak.

When you paddle well in big water, you feel good, and I remember being conscious of a grim smile on my face. I was probably also encouraging myself out loud. Ready for the unexpected, I thought I knew what I was doing. I concentrated hard on keeping squared up to the waves, but I quartered a little to port when I could—to cheat the dangerous turn I would have to make before I got to some nasty shoal water halfway between Eastern Point and Hardwood Island, which was out in front of me, a useful visual reference. I dug hard with the paddle but kept the pace steady and strength in reserve. I knew that if I started panic paddling, I would create trouble.

Despite a healthy level of nervousness about this unexpected workout, I tried to keep my body loose and stay mentally relaxed inside of the physical effort of paddling the plan I had laid out. I let the boat adjust to the offbeat rhythm of the oncoming waves and tried to avoid overreacting to any unexpected gust or swell. I knew that as long as I kept the boat from weathercocking and becoming a piece of flotsam, it would dig in and show me the way.

Just keep up some speed and let the hull stay out of the wind and carve water at the base of the waves. Every well-designed kayak has a reserve seaworthiness built into its lines—the ratios of its length, beam, and chine. You only really get to know the character of your boat in seas that activate the character of its design, testing the drawing-board idea of it.

The upwind leg was fine and built my confidence. And although it felt powerfully counterintuitive to be paddling directly away from where I wanted to go, I didn't make the mental mistake of turning prematurely. I knew if I did, I would have to turn three times—not once—through those boat-flipping troughs in order to clear the mouth of the Narrows. I watched the waves, paddled hard, and kept a mark on the north end of Hardwood Island. I reminded myself to dig hard but not flail, and when I knew I was far enough out from Bartlett Island, I wallowed fearfully through the turn I had worried about since palming myself off the cobbles of Dogfish Cove.

I could feel the unnerving roll of the swells as I went parallel to them. And I could feel the kayak heel deeply for a long, nauseating field moment until we got things right. The stern caught a few times and was wrenched the wrong way unexpectedly. I improvised strokes—ugly draws and sweeps—and, with luck, kept from going over. All through the turn, I stiffened when I needed to stay loose, but that big beam water got to me. When I missed strokes, paddling air instead of water, I could feel the boat weathercock out of my control with frightening quickness. Then I would dig hard—grabbing water any way I could—and just make sure, like a canoeist in rapids, that

I was going faster or slower than the big, gray water moving around me.

I watched Bartlett Island out of the corner of my eye and reminded myself not to finish the turn too soon, but I think in the end the decision wasn't mine. At some point I just needed to get out of the troughs and take my chances on the downwind leg. When I got squared up to the waves again, now with the wind at my back, I breathed a little easier, and the boat took over again. I had probably fought it too much through the turn, but there's a first time in every type of water.

I couldn't find the rhythm of the big waves coming at me from behind. Not only were they being driven hard by the wind into the Narrows but, somewhere underneath me, that outgoing tide was flowing strongly the other way. Running with the wind, my paddling was hit or miss at first. When I felt the wind grabbing my blades from behind, I was glad to have the paddle lash on. I waited with a minor sense of dread for the way the stern would suddenly rise and get pushed forward, with the bow cocked oddly downward.

The channel between Hardwood and Bartlett, nearly 200 foot deep in places, abuts the shallower water—sixty to eighty feet—at the mouth of the Narrows. And although it was reassuring to get closer to the familiar, often placid confines between Sawyers Cove and Eastern Point, that shallow water didn't make for easier going until I got nearly to Folly Island. Then that tightness in my gut felt good, because I didn't need it anymore. The shoreline of Bartlett came quickly back into focus and there was nothing wrong—loons floated here and there, herring gulls hung on that wind as if it were a plaything, crows flocked loudly on Folly Island.

Most days, kayaking these coastal waters is as peaceful as a walk in the woods. One of the pleasures of kayaking is to see and feel this coast from as near to sea level as you can get without swimming, to view waves and shoreline from the perspective of a loon or an eider, to ride nearly as low in the water as a cormorant, to move about with something like the freedom of a harbor seal.

From a kayak, you can look at the mountains where you walk and enrich your understanding of where you have been. You can develop a different sense of distance, the slippery feel of nautical miles, cove to cove, headland to headland, island to island, that no map reading or shore walking can convey. Of course, distances vary with the weather. In tumultuous waters, you can feel miles from home five hundred yards away from the landing you need to reach. No two paddling days are ever quite the same. From a kayak, you get a finer sense of the relation of Mount Desert's landforms, its mountains and glacial spaces, which move along with you on every paddle stroke and then tack away abruptly when you change course.

Autumn is best for paddling. By mid-October, a lot of boats are gone from their moorings at Bartletts Landing, yarded for the season, shrink-wrapped in plastic the way they store them now. A parking lot that's jammed in summer is empty. Even the Porta Potti that services the lot has been dry-docked somewhere, though presumably not shrink-wrapped. It's mostly working boats that are left, a barge of lobster bait that it's best to stay upwind of, and the venerable ferry that keeps the enviable denizens of Bartlett Island supplied with junker cars and other necessities.

Mount Desert is at its best this time of year. The island gains stature after the summer haze blows off and the relentless busyness of the tourist season burns itself out. Every day in autumn is a different season and somehow every change seems for the better. Warm days and cool days take their turns. Bad weather puts unfamiliar, migrating birds on the water. Fair weather opens doors to invigorating days in the woods or on the bare summits or paddling the coast in the blue, hazeless light that photographers and painters love. The hardwoods quickly burn their colors and pack up the idea of growth for the year. The pines and spruce and fir and cedar seem to darken, closing ranks for their winter watch. You can feel the whole North Atlantic coast, from Newfoundland to Cape Cod, clearing its decks in an orderly way for the colder half of the year. In late summer and early autumn, I feel less like a visitor and more like a potential settler.

Put in at Bartletts Landing some morning in October. Paddle through the moorings of the quiet anchorage there and then out into Bartlett Narrows, where a stiff breeze blows across the long, narrow reach of open water past the south end of Tinker Island, across the Eastern Passage to Blue Hill Bay, and then between Moose and Hardwood Islands at the mouth of the Narrows. You feel the wider, deeper water of the Gulf of Maine in that breeze. And as you paddle south, you watch the parallax of islands and recession of headlands across the surface of the ruffled water, a kayaker's unique view.

Circle Johns Island and Folly Island and then cruise the shoreline of Pretty Marsh Harbor, birding the dense spruce-fir

woods. Then paddle back across the Narrows, crows and gulls busy overhead. Here and there a monarch butterfly will flutter over the water and remind you of the season. Turn from time to time to enjoy the graceful arc of your quiet wake and to note the way Western Mountain turns behind you, vaning this way and that against your wandering course. Mark the strong flight of osprey and the bald eagles that appear out of nowhere. Watch mixed flocks of migrating warblers and nuthatches feeding high in the spruce and pine. Listen to jays and flickers *cack* in the woods and to kingfishers slinging themselves loudly across the coves of Bartlett Island. Steal up on a raccoon sifting through shellfish at the waterline, fussily inspecting mussels.

Paddle south out of the Narrows toward that shifting parallax of islands and headlands. Hardwood Island lies dead ahead, a good destination in fair weather. Then Moose Island separates itself from the southwest coast of Mount Desert. You could paddle down to it to watch sea caves forming on its inland shore. Like every island off the coast of Maine, Moose Island is found art, a mess of shatter-zone rock sheathed on its southern end with Ellsworth Schist. Great gray boulders with waterlines like boats wait along the shore with the profound patience of stone. Worn to smooth hulls painted with orange lichen, they look like they would easily float away on a high-enough tide. Somehow good second-growth woods thrive on Moose Island's thin, young soils, which you can see in cross section as you bob along the lee shore. In the spring and fall, those woods are full of migrating birds, warblers mostly, feasting on the conifer's oily seeds.

Get eye level with the roots of red spruce, white spruce, and white birch and with huge old boulders bearded with rockweed and crusted with barnacles. Note the folded bedrock slowly form-ing sea caves at the water's edge—thick, arched ledges of reddish granite eroding from underneath, spalling off in great stone flakes chiseled every winter by the silent percussion of freeze and thaw, the waste rock ground by storms and carried off, grain by grain, by the tides. Look closely and you'll see columns and sea stacks taking shape in the wet shadows.

Paddling gives you at least a small taste of the pace and char-acter of indigenous travel, since the Abenaki used sealskin and moose skin kayaks on this coast. From a kayak, you get to know intimately the terrain of water, if you will, a more complicated realm than the gray or blue expanse we see from shore. You learn that there are trails offshore, interesting paths along shorelines and between islands. Every channel, every cove, every offshore ledge or exposed reach shows you something. The pleasure of paddling is punctuated by field moments doled out by the weather and the light and the casual transit of birds and other animals. The ordinary and the extraordinary fuse easily along the shoreline of Mount Desert Island. The rhythm of paddling is another way of measuring time. Steadily paced minutes of quiet cruising slow to the molten seconds that drip from the tip of your paddle blade when you stop to observe something that catches your eye.

When paddling along the southeast shore of Bartlett Island, I enjoy morning light on waves and the silver silhouettes of common birds—gulls, loons, cormorants—just the shape of them floating in the glare, their dark forms not *on*, I noted, but *in* the silver water, *as if they had been painted there*. I admire that fine gray barnacle zone exposed on the eastern side of Bartlett, which is built half of Cadillac granite and half—divided north to south—of that ancient Ellsworth Schist. I have wonder what laws of physics and chemistry—of wave action and weathering—and of biology—of evolutionary ingenuity—create so many scalloped shapes, animate and inanimate, along the scalloped shoreline of any coast. I'll listen to chickadees and yellow-rumps in the spruce and note the solemnity of northern white cedar along the southeastern shore of Bartlett, the lattice of its bark as fine as the basketry of the Passamaquoddy and perhaps an inspiration for those artful indigenous designs.

I have a good autumn day in front of me and a fair southwest breeze and a plan to paddle, as slowly as I can, north along Bartlett's western shore, around the north end of the island—often good for spotting eagles and seafowl—and then back into the Narrows. Taken slowly, this is a good day trip—a contemplative solo paddle or, with friends, a good social outing. Although I started my outdoor life as a fisherman and hunter, I am inclined, more and more each year, to make observation the goal of hours in the field. Watching, noticing, seeing—these seem to be the proper work of the hours.

At some point on this October cruise, I found myself paddling a few feet behind a cormorant—a common sight, though the kayak let me get closer to this bird than I ordinarily do. I watched this self-possessed creature twist its head nervously back and forth, most of its oily body awash—as fishlike as seafowl gets—all neck and beak and birdy attentiveness. When I got too close, the cormorant took off in a halfhearted fashion, dragging its feet through the water, the bird a wet glossy mass, water dripping thickly off it.

Paddling in its direction, I kept coming up on this bird. Unattractive to some, the cormorant was as worthy as any creature to follow for as long as it would tolerate me. Each time I disturbed the bird, it would scuttle off and then resettle into its routine of preening and feeding, making elegant splashes when it dove, a crystal column of water rising and falling in place behind it.

A little farther on, a spotted sandpiper, already in its winter plumage, bobbed on a shelf of granite. It looked like a newly minted bird—grayish-brown, perfectly white underneath, with the long, straight bill around which the species' profile is organized. A small bird, sandpipers are dense with vivacity, stoutly delicate. Their large, dark eyes take in everything around them. They flee without alarm and quickly light elsewhere, feeding their way along the shore.

Peeping with each burst of flight, tail flicking white, this one led me to a midden of blue mussels at the base of a sea-worn cedar. The southeast shoreline of Bartlett is scalloped with these mussel coves, and at the head of this one, just opposite Folly Island, I could hear a small stream in the woods falling through some hidden crevice in a brow of moss-covered granite.

I paddled slowly that October day, feeling autumn flocking

in from the north, a thousand nameless sensations rustling in the woods and water around me. I felt like I was being passed along from one instructive form of life to another—from the cormorant to the sandpiper to the invisible stream flowing behind the mussel midden and back to the sea-worn cedar. It was darkly eyed with the worn stobs of dead branches, its twisting bark stripped and sanded to a stony sheen.

As I slowly circumnavigated Bartlett Island, I let my attention oscillate between one thing and another and felt as much a part of this *privilege of islands*—an odd phrase in my notes—as I could. When I found myself off Dogfish Point, surrounded by the unearthly breathing of the gentlest of cetaceans—the sleek blue backs of harbor porpoises arching around me on a feed—I felt that I was paddling pretty well, and that although not native to these waters, I had found an instructive *way* through them.

Paddling was another way to become intimate with the beautiful indifference in nature, to feel the keen double edge of our kinship with it and estrangement from it. The casually passionate breathing of porpoises—the raspy hunger for air you hear in that wet rush—and the shapely geometry of their swimming, the admirable fluidity of their lives, seems a gentle rebuke to any other, less graceful way of being.

Unless the wind picks up, a circumnavigation of Bartlett Island will provide you with little adventure beyond what your powers of observation can bring to life. Paddling, like walking, moves you through an extraordinary world of changing continuity, gives you detailed contact with the particularity of nature here, as well as a sense of the seamless wholeness of it. You measure time paddle stroke by paddle stroke, sometimes moving through hours and miles that put up little resistance, until something arrests your attention. Then time will briefly stand still like that crystal column of water that hangs in the air behind a diving cormorant, or like the unmoving darkness in the eye of a sandpiper before it flits off, or the mesmerizing latticework of the bark of northern white cedar, or the unspeakably graceful arc of a feeding porpoise.

I sculled the blue water off Dogfish Point until the porpoises disappeared, then paddled around a bit in the space of their absence before moving off north along the west shore of Bartlett Island.

> *Nature proceeds little by little from things lifeless to animal life in such a way that it is impossible to determine the exact line of demarcation. . . . So, in the sea, there are certain objects concerning which one would be at a loss to determine whether they be animal or vegetable.*
>
> —ARISTOTLE,
> *HISTORIA ANIMALIUM*, BOOK VIII

LONG LEDGE—

Walking Out to Sea

By early July, eiders are alongshore with fledglings that were hatched on outer islands. Flocks of females herd chicks in the quiet coves where the young can learn the business of being eiders. Gray birds with striped faces, the young of the year float high, barely denting the water. The females tend them closely, keeping downy flotillas together just beyond where the small waves break in a mess of knotweed. The chicks paddle about tentatively, pecking at the quietly surging water, imitating the way the mature ducks feed.

As they ride the slack-tide wavelets of Bennet Cove, you can see the chicks learning to trust their buoyancy in the gentle wash of low tide. These local eiders will spend their entire lives keeping time with the waters of the Gulf of Maine. And although they will grow to be quite strong on the wing, and eventually fly with the impressive, stiff-winged speed of their elders, they will first learn to set their roots deep into the cold coastal waters that will feed them for a lifetime.

I came down the Wonderland Trail, famous among birders, trying not to get too distracted by the warblers and nuthatches in the spruce, the white-throats calling from a pitch pine bald over which mourning doves clattered toward woods where flickers and hairy woodpeckers hammered away. I left the trail and followed a little-used path through the woods to the quiet shore of Bennet Cove.

Walk soft on the moss, crouch under the low dead limbs of the conifers, surprising hermit thrush or ovenbirds a log or two away. Look into their wild eyes, darkly disappointed at the success of your stealth, the rare failure of their native wariness. Steal up on the seaside sparrows hidden in the beach rose and mallow just above the spring-tide wrack line—song sparrows, swamp sparrows, maybe savannah and Lincoln's sparrows. These quick birds, artful at staying just out of view, rarely perch on an outer branch long enough for you to parse the subtle diagnostic features of their faces and wings.

Before you step into an early morning hour on Bennet Cove, changing it with the presence of your curiosity, sit down on a sea-polished log abandoned at the wrack line along with crumpled lobster traps, broken toggles, and tangled cordage. Enjoy the subtle way this part of the coast comes to light in the morning. Watch from behind the beach rose and flowering mallow full of sparrows, with those thrush and ovenbirds in the woods behind you, and for a moment you will swear you can see what time is—the gift of it so clearly at hand—just as you might glimpse it at the Ship Harbor channel, and on rough water off Dogfish Cove, or up among the beautiful array of erratic boulders on the long south slope of Penobscot Mountain, or listening for whales in the fog out on the Gulf of Maine. There are many dawns on Mount Desert Island. Here at Bennet Cove you can watch a day glide into place, stirred by a little wind and the gentle lap of slack high tide on shore and announced by the uninterpretable cries of gulls.

Beautiful as they are, these tidal places are often moody and strange. Sometimes you can feel the bittersweet tang of your mortality rubbing up against a beachhead of infinity. In odd moments you feel privy to and alienated from whatever *being* is. The primal look and feel, the sounds and odors of tidal zones can stimulate that sense of the uncanny, that thrilling but unsettling awareness of being *shipwrecked* in nature—like Crusoe on his island— home but not home. Of course, you can't spend too many minutes indulging such a sensation, but quiet moments on the shore of these tidal coves will mesmerize you as surely as the soft waves of the Aegean stirred the Presocratics to wonder about the nature of nature.

The sights and sounds of the littoral hone the hours to a razor edge. The tangible and the transcendental fuse in some recognizable form—in the profile of an osprey half-hidden in a spruce, in the gray face of a sparrow just visible in a thicket of beach rose, in the cockiness of a herring gull brashly perched on a smashed lobster trap.

From the head of Bennet Cove you'll see the dark shape of Long Ledge emerging into another day, the black rock another gnomon of another sundial in a landscape where daylight is

almost always throwing telling shadows across the long back of
some species of bedrock pointed seaward. A granite ledge of complicated structure, the wet, black length of Long Ledge organizes
tidal energies here in Bennet Cove and out beyond the mouth of
it. I've come here to watch it a hundred times.

The inner ledge protects the head of the cove, making it a
low-energy upper tidal zone, in the parlance of marine ecology.
Any textbook will tell you that the life of a tidal zone is determined primarily by substrate and wave energy. The poetics of
the tidal zone—which for the layman is readily apparent in the
appealing diversity of life you find there—is, at root, a function
of energy transfer at a complicated, overlapping marine/terres-
trial border made of sea water and rock, crushed shell and funky,
organic mud.

The tide rises and falls quietly in the upper cove, slowly bulging
up toward the spruce-fir woods out of which black-and-white warblers and northern parulas call nearly constantly some days in summer. High tides leave necklaces of wrack lines on a short cobble beach
where snowshoe hares and raccoons forage. The latter, I think, are
responsible for the sea urchins I sometimes find deep in the nearby
woods—perfectly unmarred shells left on mossy stumps.

The inner half of Long Ledge, on which a mixed colony of
gulls is almost always busy, divides the mouth of Bennet Cove in
two. A narrow tidal gut separates the inner ledge from the mainland. This gut is a textbook illustration of the mid-tidal zone, a
quiet place at slack tides but a strong tidal stream on the changes.
The mainland littoral is a slippery mess of rockweed and knotweed impossible to walk on, but as the tide recedes you can shuffle through the channel toward the outer half of Long Ledge.

The thing to do at Bennet Cove is to catch the half-tide falling early on a summer morning. Leave yourself enough time to explore the quiet head of the cove. Go back into the woods to wander the granite balds that are hidden there. Then, as the tide streams seaward with increasing quickness, follow it out to sea as far as you can go. Walk carefully to minimize the disturbance of your passing. Head toward Long Ledge as if it were a cairn that marked the end of a trail.

Although not much more than a mile there and back, this is as fine a walk as you can take on Mount Desert Island. Like everything else that makes a living here, give yourself over for a day to a tidal schedule. Pace yourself to the rhythms that keep the dulse, kelp, and sea grass pulsing in place. Take a hint from all the filter-feeding forms of life at your feet and let your senses and consciousness filter-feed on the tide. The more slowly you walk, the more you become a tidal creature, and the longer the trail to Long Ledge will be.

The outer part of Long Ledge is cut off from the mainland at high tide. All but the high, black fin of rock that comprises the ten-foot summit of Long Ledge is claimed by the gulf. In heavy weather, Long Ledge is a dangerous place. Even in fair weather, the complicated waters around it are a navigational hazard for all but the most shallow-drafted boats. Seasoned locals sometimes shortcut the channel between it and the mainland at high tide, looking pretty cocky as they ease over that hidden cobble bar with just enough freeboard, but most boats stay on the gulf side of the bell buoy that marks the Western Way into Southwest Harbor.

In the days before navigational aids and accurate charts, Long Ledge claimed its share of hulls and lives. Around 1740, *The Grand*

Design, a ship of two or three hundred tons out of Ulster bound for Pennsylvania, was driven onto the ledge in a storm. It's not hard to imagine how quickly a wooden-hulled ship would have been ground to bits on the black granite of Long Ledge and how difficult it would have been for passengers and crew to make it the short distance to shore.

Hundreds of lives were lost that day in this usually placid place. The little-known event is one of many facts about the rigors of colonial life hidden in the history of this coast. Many of those who did not drown in the ferocious water or on the black rocks perished ashore from injuries, exhaustion, hunger, and thirst. To come to Mount Desert by shipwreck in 1740 was to come to a dismal place. On board *The Grand Design* were wealthy settlers as well as poor bondsmen and -women. The salvage was a strange affair of silk dresses and sodden potatoes. The survivors traded Irish linen for food from the Native Americans who found them. These were likely Penobscot or Passamaquoddy, for whom Mount Desert was a bountiful fishery for half the year. They helped the survivors make it to a fledgling Irish settlement down the coast at Damariscotta. Most apparently stayed in Maine, adding their hardiness and luck—survivors of the wreck of one grand design and inheritors of an accidental future—to the Yankee stock that learned to thrive on this coast in the eighteenth and nineteenth centuries.

At high tide, Long Ledge is remote enough from human disturbance for seals to haul out on the same rocks on which *The Grand Design* foundered, and it is not unusual to see a bald eagle perched on the crest of its algae-blackened granite. At low tide in summer, you just shuffle shin-deep or knee-deep across the cobble bar if you want and come back across before the tide comes fully in.

Life came out of the sea, evolving by slow degrees in the rich stew of tidal zones. A walk to Long Ledge is an easy way for the layman to slosh through that scientific fact. In the vegetative and marine life of the tidal zones, you can clearly see a repository of evolutionary strategy, a reservoir of life forms and biological responses to constantly changing physical and chemical conditions. What would put more of a premium on the idea of adaptation than a realm, like the tidal zone, where the conditions of life are *never* quite the same—not tide to tide, day to day, season to season? Walking to Long Ledge, you have the genius of evolution at your feet, the currents out of which life arose on this planet casually streaming around your shins.

Stare down at sunlit tidal pools where periwinkles graze small rocks that look like seamounts when you shift your sense of scale. Admire the way eelgrass lies seaward, a perfect compass of the tide. Watch the bladder wrack and knotweed come to life in moving water. Parse as best you can the filmy dulse and the green, purple, and brown seaweeds. Walk carefully around dense beds of blue mussels. Enjoy the otherworldly palette of marine colors—watery shades of blue, green, red, and brown for which we have no words. Reach into the strange vegetation and watch cunners, sculpin, and several varieties of crab scoot from those sea grasses and seaweeds.

It's easy to become a citizen of the woods if you spend enough time there. But in the tidal zone, it's as if you have the pleasure of walking on another planet, a chance to encounter how fluid the idea of life is. This walk to Long Ledge is a way of walking out to sea, a way of keenly feeling the productive, competitive tension between the terrestrial and the marine at the height of summer. Walking a tidal zone is only superficially like the more familiar practice of river walking; tidal flows have a far more complicated hydrology and a more diverse and variable biology than the flows of rivers. Even the gentlest tidal current feels strange twisting around your shins, not flowing insistently downstream like a river. However much they meander and braid, rivers flow famously down to the sea. But these shallow, shifting tidal waters are the sea—the pulsing, swirling edge of it.

While studying the life on the landward side of the bar, I hear the heavy splash of an osprey diving successfully on what is at least a foot-long sculpin—a shorthorn sculpin, I guess later, thumbing through a field guide I've dragged around the wet rocks for years. The sound of the osprey's dive, the rude *thock* of the capture fifty feet away, is an emphatic assertion of predatory prerogative here in shallow tidal waters where life is, at all points, a gamble. The osprey adjusts its grip on the arc of fish and flies back, a little heavily, to a nest hidden in the woods at the head of Bennet Cove, from which I emerged hours ago.

Eventually, this broad cobble bar that separates the outer ledge from the mainland becomes shallow enough for wading. As I slosh across, I note that the water on the east side is deep and looks good for fishing. And the fishing is good—a greater blackbacked gull grabs a green crab, whacks it on the rocks, then flies up with it and drops the doomed thing on the rocks. The blackback studiously picks the legs off the crab—one of the first lessons a gull must learn—and then feasts deep into the heart of it.

The osprey comes back to fish again but is put off by my being on the bar. After circling this choice spot, where the tide drains off in two directions around the inner edge of Long Ledge, it heads off elsewhere. The herring gulls and black-backs also keep their distance at first but can't resist the opportunity of all the food-rich niches now exposed.

These outer tidal zones, more exposed to heavy weather, harbor different life than what's in the quiet recesses of Bennet Cove. Rough-textured sea colander thrives in these rougher waters, along with the long-vesicled *edentata* bladder wrack and something that looks like edible kelp. There are colonies of pinkish-white tubers that might either be rubbery or panpipe bryozoans, which, although they look like vegetation, are classified as a form of animal life. There are whelks and other mollusks that I do not find closer to shore—many rough barnacles in addition to the more familiar northern rock barnacle. I walk among sourweeds and whipweeds, ribbon weeds and frayed weeds, filmy dulse and Irish moss and leaf weeds.

I find a horsetail kelp gripping a horse mussel—a nice efficiency of language. The mussel is covered with periwinkles and two rough barnacles and has a brushy and a flat-veined seaweed attached to it. The tidal zone is rich with such fistfuls of life, symbiotic communities, entanglements of life forms and strategies. Stirred by the tides, chance and necessity play their game here, too. Evolution is an art and the tidal zone a gallery.

The poetics of life on Long Ledge is the poetics of surviving in extreme conditions. Here every life form clinging tenaciously to its niche is a vivid embodiment of the biological will to live. On Long Ledge, beautiful and desolate, life seems to say, *I will do anything, be anything, just to thrive, just to have my time in the sun, just to have a throw at being.* Of course, the forces and conditions that craft any successful adaptation also craft its competition. A shorthorn sculpin is handed over, in pieces, to an osprey's young, or a colony of kelp is ripped from its holdfasts in a storm.

Once across the bar and out on Long Ledge proper, you've gained a fine vantage. You can get up on a smooth hump of granite that rises above a chaos of rock and wrack, driftwood and detritus that changes on every tide. This is where bald eagles perch at high tide, overlooking a cove you cannot see from shore. This is where those folks from Ulster foundered. In its own way, this hump of rock is another of Mount Desert's summits.

Out here you feel like you have gotten measurably closer to the Duck Islands, and you have a fine view of the Eastern Passage into Blue Hill Bay. You can see the near shore of Long Island and the pronounced notch at the end of Rich Head, its easternmost extension. You can think of days spent walking the pristine south shore of Long Island after a good dockside lunch in Frenchboro. Beyond that south shore of Long Island, there is nothing but the Gulf of Maine and the Atlantic Ocean, except for a tantalizing speck of granite known as Mount Desert Rock, the outermost island along the coast of Maine. On Long Ledge, among the driftwood and gulls and the sun, listening to the complicated wash of the tide, you feel you are at another trailhead even though you cannot go a step farther. Turn your attention back to Mount Desert Island itself. From out on Long Ledge you have a good view of the island's mountainous profile, its rugged, sea-worn structure: Norumbega, Sargent, Penobscot, Pemetic, Cadillac, and Champlain—the peaks that make Mount Desert Island such a striking landmark.

But when you are out on Long Ledge, watch your reveries and the tide closely. Measure time not by minutes or hours but by inches—the depth of water rattling over the cobble bar after the tide has turned. Watch the tidal flow coming back from all directions. Because of the complex structure of the ledge, the incoming tide is many-headed, a hydra of insistent energy shaping water to its will, swirling and snapping and flowing in its syrupy way, inching in, deepening.

As you come back across the bar—shin-deep, knee-deep, or waist-deep in the cold water, depending on how long you have lingered on Long Ledge—enjoy the complicated reassertion of the incoming tide. Admire the way the late-afternoon sun hits the curling waves on the west side of the channel, the way the light is refracted into a dense colony of kelp being lifted by those sunlit waves as they enjoy—there is no other word for it—the wavelike form lent to them by the surging, deepening water.

Wade back to a shoreline disappearing under the incoming tide.

*There is such an abundance of birds
of different sorts that one could not
imagine if he had not seen them. . . .*

—SAMUEL DE CHAMPLAIN,
IN THE GULF OF MAINE, 1604

DOWN EAST—

Imagining Birds

The Porcupine Islands come out of the dark like ships swung-to
on their anchors. Their rock hulls creak softly against the authority of an incoming tide as thick ranks of close-hauled evergreens
luff in a modest southeasterly. Herring gulls ply the cool, late-
September air. Gangs of crows converse. The tide stirs against
dock pilings as you sip coffee in the company of the sooty house
sparrows that live in the shrubbery of Bar Harbor's alleyways.

Work begins in the dark at Bar Harbor long before the tourist day begins, the bobbing cabin lights of idling lobster boats a
counterpart to a few bold stars that oversee the predawn hour.
What's left of a working waterfront, hemmed in by hotels and
concessions, services a small fleet that clings to this magnificent
anchorage. When a boat comes to the dock for plastic bins of

reeking bait and other necessities, captain and sternman do the work quickly. Routine requires little talk. Watching, you feel like a fool for having nothing to do.

Each boat rumbles away slowly through the moorings—more beautiful than the yachts it passes—stern settling down with each increase in throttle as a craft that is somehow both stocky and sleek swings to the well-worn heading that will take it past Bald Porcupine Island toward Egg Rock and the mouth of Frenchman Bay. As they depart, their cabin lights shine on the crests of the broad, low wake characteristic of these most seaworthy of working boats.

Then dawn dawns with no more fanfare than the tide turns, a gray sky briefly tinged with rose and blue that a good painter would remember but not make too much of. This last summer morning breaks fair on a day that will eventually go overcast and roughen into autumn before our eyes.

I'm here among a hundred or so others, passengers on the Maine Audubon Society's annual pelagic-bird excursion, a dream come true for anyone who wants to witness the offshore natural life of the Down East coast during a season not only of great beauty but of intense migration. In late summer and throughout the autumn, this coast is rich with arrival and departure—from the great flocks of eiders gathering to winter here to the fragile panes of monarch butterflies darting over these cold coastal waters toward their winter roosts in Mexico.

I can't think of a finer way to move from one season to another than to leave Bar Harbor at the very end of summer, coast Down East to Grand Manan at the mouth of the Bay of Fundy by way of Petit Manan and Machias Seal Island, and return at evening in rising seas, Schoodic Peninsula frothing, to find autumn occupying the slopes of Mount Desert.

I perch in the rear of the upper deck on the starboard side, eager for a day of observation. Birders are often the butt of jokes, but I find the intensity of this voyage's collective interest in seeing birds and marine life heartening. There are naturalists on board from the College of the Atlantic in Bar Harbor and from Allied Whale, which conducts research on whales in the Gulf of Maine. Spotters from the Maine Audubon Society help identify the more difficult birds. I've spent four years parsing offshore birds on my own, enjoying as I always do the trial and error of coming to understand what I am seeing at a pace that suits me. This bracing day on open water turns out to be an extraordinary opportunity to watch and learn.

The town of Bar Harbor quickly recedes as the boat follows the arc of the Porcupines. If you spend enough time there, Mount Desert can come to seem like a mainland, a world unto itself, but as soon as you are out on Frenchman Bay, you see it as an island again, light on the water somehow, riding any tide with the buoyancy of all islands.

Mount Desert turns as the boat turns, its interior ridges and valleys coming into view as you follow that sweeping course along the southern faces of Sheep, Burnt, and Long Porcupine Islands. With every change of heading, Mount Desert rudders about, the fine art of glacial sculpting shown to good advantage by the shifting perspective of your departure. By the time you are passing the great stonework of the well-named Ironbound Island, you have fine views of the way the overturned hull of Champlain Mountain is set against the hull of Dorr, with Cadillac rising behind them. The structure of each is drawn in distinct relief, the stress of their geological formation soft-ened by weathering and wind-pruned vegetation.

Out on Frenchman Bay, you get glimpses not only of the mountains but of the graceful spaces between them, that figure and ground of glacial scouring and retreat, that profound reci-procity of natural forces so fundamental to the look of things here. Then, as you approach Egg Rock, the great headlands and landmarks of the south coast of Mount Desert show themselves facing dawn on the gulf to good effect. Some days, you have to leave Mount Desert to see it, take in this recessional of glacial land forms, those great curves of rock and space, one behind the other, smooth as time.

Following the fading wake of the lobster boats, we pass the tidal ledges and jumbled high ground of Egg Rock, a great attractor for birds and seals and, with its squat lighthouse, the principal beacon for mariners making Frenchman Bay in bad weather. This time of year, Egg Rock is surrounded by large rafts of eiders, resident birds joined by migrants from farther up the coast—as far as Labrador and Newfoundland—that winter here in large numbers. Herring gulls and laughing gulls stitch the air, along with ring-billed and greater black-backed gulls. Black guillemots bob about. Occasionally you notice the unmistakable silhouette of a loon. Ospreys and bald eagles pass overhead. White-winged scoters hustle back and forth, their wingbeats quicker than that of eiders, their angle of attack not as flat. In autumn as in spring, this coast is woven with the lives of birds. By the time a red sun is thumb high, we are clear of Schoodic Point and headed Down East.

It doesn't take long to get from the Schoodic Peninsula to Petit Manan, a low-lying shelf of rock islanded just off the peninsula of the same name and one of the rare nesting sites for puffins, murres, and razorbills. The island is home to a slender candle of a lighthouse, an elegantly spare, 125-foot granite tower capped with black ironwork. The flocks of nesting seabirds you can see here in June and July are long gone by late September. As in Frenchman Bay, gulls and eiders and scoters feed in the tidal waters around the island or glean shellfish from among its rocks and rockweeds.

Beyond Petit Manan, a modest sea runs gray and white as that leading edge of autumn comes down the coast bringing birds. It was Samuel de Champlain who first recorded the diverse bird-life of this region. In the spring of 1604, on his second voyage to North America, the Frenchman explored the southern coast of Nova Scotia, a hundred miles east of here, and gave us the first bird list for *l'Acadie*, the Acadia for which Acadia National Park is named.

Champlain was exploring what he named the Sea-Wolf or Seal Islands—*"Isles aux loups marins"*—off the southwest tip of Nova Scotia near the eastern side of the mouth of the *La Baye Française* (the Bay of Fundy). He reports finding an "infinite number" of cormorants on what is now called Green Island, near Cape Sable. Always foraging, his men filled a cask with eggs. A little farther east he reports that on one island "we saw so great a number of birds called *tangueux* that we killed them easily with a stick. On another we found the shore completely covered with seals, whereof we took as many as we wished."

Those *tangueux* Champlain's men clubbed were great auk, the largest North Atlantic alcid, the last known specimens of which were killed for their eggs and skins—on behalf of Victorian collectors—off Iceland in 1844. A bit farther on, still among the Seal Islands, the French explorer reports on what he declared, with unusual emphasis in his matter-of-fact journal, to be an unimaginable abundance and diversity of birds. He identifies "cormorants, ducks of three kinds, snow-geese, murres, wild geese, puffins, snipe, fish-hawks, and other birds of prey, sea-gulls, plover of two or three kinds, herons, herring gulls, curlews, turnstones, divers, loons, eiders, ravens, cranes, and other kinds unknown to me."

Except for the doomed great auk, Champlain observed the same rich diversity of birds that can still be seen, though in much-diminished numbers, along a coast he carefully mapped during his explorations of 1604, 1605, and 1606: great and double-crested cormorants, eiders, scoters, loons, Canada geese, eagles, puffins, turkey vultures, Leach's and Wilson's storm-petrels, great blue herons, greater black-backed gulls, herring gulls, laughing gulls, ring-billed gulls, black guillemots, dovekies, razorbills, murres, osprey, ravens, crows, and others.

Beyond what he manages to name, Champlain must have seen the three terns we still see—the common, arctic, and roseate—as well as shearwaters, gannets, fulmars, phalaropes, and such—widely distributed and far-traveling species. Some—arctic terns, fulmars, and storm-petrels—are among the longest-distance migratory species on earth; others, like the greater shearwater, are species that breed in the far South Atlantic and winter in the Northern Hemisphere.

This day of observation is an homage to the birdlife of the Gulf of Maine and, except for the bulky form of fulmars—thick-bodied tubenoses—I see every bird I've seen over the years during one long, mesmerizing voyage. We pass birds while slowly underway or gather them when the boat is throttled down to hold its place against the wind and waves. There are small skeins of razorbills and, occasionally, puffins, both species flying with the distinctive profile and rapid wingbeat of alcids. Great flocks of herring gulls and black-backed gulls come to the chum slick off the stern. Among them are a few lesser black-backed gulls, rarer to see. Black-legged kittiwakes appear among the gulls, another mark of a new season. Occasionally we see migrating passerines, such as rusty blackbirds, along with migrating monarch butterflies. But seabirds are the main attraction, species not rare in numbers but rare to see.

Nothing lives more remotely than seabirds. Nothing takes us beyond our terrestrial prejudices like these pelagic birds, which, having evolved or adapted to live largely at sea, use land so sparingly. Shearwaters, petrels, skuas, fulmars, jaegers, phalaropes, razorbills, puffins, murres, gannets, terns—unfamiliar birds with fabulous names—represent forms of life that embrace the simple fact we all learned in fifth grade: that most of the earth is not earth but water.

Like others, I have learned to identify pelagic birds glimpse by glimpse, trip by trip, over years, usually on whale-watch excursions. To a novice observer, the appearance of pelagics on open water is so unpredictable and their presence so fleeting that you have to practice seeing them come in and out of view just as *something* chipped from the gray horizon, hard on the move *somewhere*, before you can begin to grapple with identifying them. You scan and scan—sometimes with your naked eye and some of the time through the narrow field of binoculars—until some sourceless movement catches your eye, the merest suggestion of some form of life poised, flying fast between the gray sky and the gray sea. The neck-straining business of parsing warblers in the spruce-fir canopy is nothing compared to the challenge of taking in the form and flight of a seabird intently on its way elsewhere.

Eventually, you learn to see those small, skittering forms that swing in off the stern as storm-petrels. That stout-bodied, low-flying bird crossing the bow on a diagonal two hundred yards out is a shearwater. Those high-flying, long-winged, pointed forms are gannets. That flashing in the sunlight is terns.

But even if you are a quick study, it takes experience and practice to parse Wilson's storm-petrels from Leach's, greater shearwaters from sooty shearwaters and the occasional Cory's, arctic terns from common terns or the rarer roseates. Between sightings of these extraordinary birds, you can enjoy the stoicism of gray seals, the sleek travel of Atlantic white-sided dolphins, and the casual surfacing of humpback, fin, and minke whales.

This time of year, you don't have to get far offshore before you start seeing northern gannets, the most common harbingers of this more exotic birdlife and the largest seabirds along the North Atlantic coast. Soul-stirring flights of them cruise quickly in a variety of directions. A large bird with long, slender, swept-back wings, the gannet is a familiar coastal bird that breeds on the Gaspé Peninsula, in the Gulf of St. Lawrence, and off the north coast of Prince Edward Island and the east coast of Newfoundland. Adults are uncommon in summer, though nonbreeding young stray south. Like the scoters and other seafowl, breeding gannets shift south and east along the North Atlantic coast for the nonbreeding half of the year.

Terns attract the eye, even at a great distance, flashing in the sun when they hover and feed. Flying, they gleam in and out of view quickly. Nothing about a tern suggests lingering. Their form is as elegant as bird morphology gets, combining as it does the grace and quickness of swallows with the hardiness of gulls. Their hovering is extraordinary. Terns somehow grip enough air with rapid beating of their slender, bent wings, tails scissored open, heads and bills angled purposefully at the water below. Their plunge, though from only ten feet above the water, is as impressive as that of an osprey from a hundred.

Strong and agile, though they look delicate against an oceanic background, terns don't offer you long looks except when they have gathered over a school of baitfish driven to the surface by predators. In passing, they fly with rapid wingbeats, coursing easily on the air, casually slicing lift and air speed with those angled wings. Fast as they are, their flight is rarely linear. They don't feint about in the air like swallows, but they travel with far more indirection than a gull or a shearwater. No bird I know, swallows included, changes direction as deftly—and unpredictably—as a tern or hovers in so perfectly calculating a way.

Greater shearwaters appear with increasing frequency as you get offshore, most often one bird at a time. You occasionally see them sitting ducklike on the water, but most often you will find them flying hard and low, shearing through the troughs of waves as their name suggests they do. Compact of body and long and shapely of wing, shearwaters have the form and look of serviceable oceanic travelers. They are clearly built to live their lives across long distances in an unfathomable isolation—not to mention in weather no human being could endure.

On patrol, shearwaters seem as much a part of the ocean as any marine life I have seen, more intimate with the roily surface of the sea over which they skim than any other seabird. They seem very nearly a metamorphosis of the shape of gray waves. In a myth, they would be messengers, an aesthetic creation of the ceaselessly shifting surface of the sea. They are clearly shaped to travel incessantly and, in traveling, to shear waves so gracefully you cannot tell which form imitates which—the moving curves of wind-driven water or the eccentric sweep of this great bird's crooked wing.

All pelagic species seem strangely comfortable in the austere, offshore world, *at home* with what to the human mind is the strangeness of the sea. The uniqueness of these ocean-adapted birds can be seen with the naked eye, each species beautifully strange—original in form and vigorous in flight—and evolved to be a success in as austere an environment as one could imagine.

Sailors, of course, read much meaning in seabirds. Columbus used them mercilessly on his first voyage to mean whatever he needed them to mean, using the opportunity of any bird to signify to his men that land was near—no matter how far out at sea his flotilla was. An experienced sailor who knew better, Columbus claimed that every shearwater, tropic bird, or frigate bird that came within sight of his little fleet was a sign of land. Although such birds do frequent the waters of the continental shelf, seabirds mostly signify the sea.

Even the Puritan leader John Winthrop, who was not given to observing or admiring nature for its own sake, listed the presence of seabirds at midocean as one of the most notable facts of his voyage—across these very waters—to the New World in 1630. In the middle of the North Atlantic, just past the longitude of the most western of the Azores, he stopped to note the four most remarkable things about his ocean crossing. One was "that all the waye we came we sawe fowles flyinge & swimminge, when we had no land neere by 200 leagues."

Today, spotters frequently sight pomarine jaegers, a seasonal migrant. The "pom yager," as the spotters call it, is a barrel-chested, crossbow of a bird with a shorter wingspan than a gannet but larger than a shearwater. Agile as a tern, it is as stocky as a skua. Quick as a falcon and patient as a hawk, jaegers are often referred to as the raptors of the open ocean. Its scooped shoulders and distinctive, spatulate tail gives its authoritative flight an elegant, scissoring aspect. To my eye, the jaeger does not fly with the forceful, long-distance wingbeat of a gannet or with the graceful effortlessness of a shearwater. It is a hunting bird that lives up to its German name *Jäger* and in summer pursues small mammals and birds of the Arctic tundra regions. Jaegers take their talents, which include scavenging and poaching from other birds, offshore in winter. It is a notorious pirate of the fish other birds have captured. On this excursion, we get good looks at these hunters all day, up close and in the middle distance, dark birds and white morphs and some juveniles.

By late afternoon, we have made Machias Seal Island, a rugged outpost near the unmarked seam where the Gulf of Maine meets the Bay of Fundy. At high tide, Machias Seal from the south looks like two islands. It is the site of a sturdy granite lighthouse and a well-weathered coastal station that flies the American and

Canadian flags. We can see North Island in the near distance and the great basaltic cliffs of the south coast of Grand Manan farther off.

On Champlain's 1607 map, Machias Seal Island is called *Isle aux Perroquetz*, Island of Sea Parrots, for the puffins that nest there in June and July, packed on guano-stained rocks alongside razorbills and common murres and underneath the graceful comings and goings of arctic terns.

I first came out to Machias Seal several years ago on the long haul from Jonesport. That was in July, when the air is strangely, uncomfortably alive with birds here. In summer, you can see densities of nesting pelagics as John James Audubon saw them off the coast of Labrador in 1833, when he went seeking birds to collect and paint: "[W]e every now and then saw them around the vessel, now floating on the swelling wave, now disappearing under the bow, diving with the swiftness of thought, and sometimes rising on wing and flying swiftly, but low, over the sea." At the sites he visited, Audubon found puffins "so numerous as actually to cover the water to the extent of half an acre or more."

In breeding season there do indeed seem to be "clouds of Puffins" in the air at Machias Seal Island, adults busy bringing fish to their young. And the "loud croaking noise" they make, a weird, elemental cry, is as memorable as the sight of so many of these distinctive birds gathered in one place. The feeding of young by adults is constant, the air a confusion of awkward, fluttery landings and laborious takeoffs. The sound of thick, strong wingbeats mixing with the otherworldly cries of these birds will haunt you for days and get into your dreams. Puffins, razorbills, and murres are striking birds—iconic in their strong profiles—but coming to land is clearly a risky necessity. One can easily imagine Champlain's men battering great auks—ungainly cousin to the puffin—at their will. In summer, Machias Seal Island is the eye of the needle for the next generation of these birds.

The flight of the puffin is deceptively fast for a chunky, large-headed bird with relatively short, broad wings—"firm, generally direct, now and then pretty well sustained" in Audubon's description. And although the puffin is often promoted on postcards and souvenirs as a quintessentially cute bird, the effect of observing it closely is to enlarge your sense of how distinctive pelagic birdlife is, how remote from self-serving anthropomorphic concerns its austere natural history makes it. When you have the privilege to see them up close and watch them about their nest-tending, you see that puffins are not cute at all, but starkly other.

As was true at Petit Manan, the nesting birds are long gone, though we have been seeing small flocks of puffins and razorbills on the wing all along the coast. Today Machias Seal is under the dominion of several peregrine falcons and a merlin, which mercilessly hunt migrating warblers. Of course, gulls of every variety flock to the island in large numbers, and seals and porpoises cruise the tidal waters. On land, water is the "great attractor" for *bios*, for life. On open water, the role of the elements is reversed, and any speck of rock will bring to it every passing form of life. Raptors and scavengers alike know these island refuges as well as lions and hyenas know waterholes on the Serengeti.

So we watch for a while, rocking in a sea that runs strong enough to burst white around the ledges. We listen over the intercom to our captain chatting with the lighthouse-keeping crew— sharing information on weather and wildlife is one of the principal social obligations on the coast of Maine. Shearwaters pass, and jaegers. All the while the peregrines assert the prerogative of their hunting prowess. In the middle of nowhere, we seem to be at the center of something.

We push on beyond Machias Seal and get a closer look at Grand Manan, that great flat rock of an island that oversees the western entrance to the Bay of Fundy. Underway, we encounter flocks of greater shearwaters, maybe thirty birds in each, flying just over the waves and another flock on the water. We see solitary and small flocks of the diminutive Manx shearwaters. Terns, kittiwakes, a Leach's storm-petrel—offshore birdlife keeps coming, forming in the gray air, disappearing.

We cruise the Grand Manan Bank for a final reward, which the Gulf of Maine grants us—a right whale, rarest of the North Atlantic whale species, one of maybe 350 individuals left in the North Atlantic. The sight of this whale's strangely shaped head, the broad, bullish disturbance of its surfacing, is a rare glimpse of the poignant persistence of all things, all forms of life, to be, to survive, to go on. The right whale surfaces a second time, farther out from us, one last glimpse of rarity—the black body of a whale in a gray sea.

Coming back, we follow the track of Samuel de Champlain's first approach to Mount Desert Island. On September 2, 1604, Champlain set out from Sieur de Monts' ill-chosen settlement on an island in the St. Croix River, now boundary water between the United States and Canada, in a *patache*—a narrow vessel manned by a dozen sailors and accompanied by two *sauvages*, Micmac perhaps. He anchored for three days at the mouth of the river, waiting out bad weather, and then steered slowly south past Grand

Manan, the name of which derives from the Micmac language for "great island." Skirting an offshore fog bank, he sailed west, close enough to shore to observe the rocky complexity of a coast that he carefully charted on his invaluable maps: "Continuing our course along the coast we made this day some twenty-five leagues, and past a great number of islands, sand banks, shoals, and rocks which in some places project more than four leagues out to sea"—the same twenty-five leagues we cover today.

He named the islands that picket the coast from Little Machias Bay to Great Wass Island *Les Isles Rangées* for the orderly way they ranged out from the coast. It was Great Wass Island, which reaches southeast into the Gulf of Maine from Jonesport and Beals Island, that forced him "four leagues out to sea." In Champlain's journals and on his maps, Great Wass is called *Isle aux Corneilles*, for the great flocks of crows that can still be found there, mixed with ravens, osprey, and bald eagles. Champlain used the island's prominent, tide-whitened southern shore as a landmark when sailing between Cape Cod and the Bay of Fundy on his return trip in 1604 and again in 1605 and 1606 when he made extended excursions to Cape Cod. Champlain typically set his course from Grand Manan to *Isle aux Corneilles* and then, keeping Mount Desert in sight, to Isle au Haut—which he also named—and on to the cape.

Although Champlain was in the vanguard of the European invasion of a world that needed no discovering, he seems moved at times in his writings by the beauty of densely forested islands, bold headlands, intricately carved coves, inlets, and channels whose navigation changed with every rise and fall of tide and every shift of wind. Then as now, no moment on this coast was ever the same. He was befogged by the same obscurity that shrouds many summer days offshore. I doubt that the rope of his sounding lead ever dried out.

Champlain charted this coast well and described the landscape and its wildlife with an attentive eye. A superb cartographer, Champlain keenly observed coastal landforms, noted currents and tides with care, kept a sharp eye on the weather, and listed, along the way, every tree and animal and bird he could name. When he was not busy with the navigational challenges of often-foggy coastal waters, he was taking stock of what we now call the biodiversity of this great marine ecosystem. He named what he saw as best he could—trees, birds, animals—and absorbed a sense of native lifeways that was invaluable to French explorers and settlers in later years. He composed extended descriptions of Canada geese, red-winged blackbirds, passenger pigeons, horseshoe crabs, black skimmers, porpoises, and wild turkeys. The fabulous natural life of North America *was* a new world to Europeans.

Champlain's well-known map of 1612 was profusely illustrated with the great diversity of natural life he found along the coast of North America—seals, beaver, bears, martens, raccoons, muskrats, foxes, striped bass, salmon, sturgeon, tubers, chestnuts, mollusks, sculpins. He marveled at forests the likes of which Europe had not seen for a thousand years and inventoried the arboreal wealth of the coast—pines, firs, spruce, oaks, birch, maples. Champlain sailed these Down East waters before there was a Massachusetts Bay Colony for him to be down east of, and he saw this magnificent coast as many of us would like to have seen it.

A light rain starts up when we are an hour or so out from Bar

Harbor, the kind of rain it feels good to stand out in, keeping faith with a day of getting weathered, a day of giving one's consciousness over to the life of things out on the gulf. A new sea builds as we pass Petit Manan, Champlain's *Isle de Sasinou*. The coast whitens. We stay well off Schoodic Island—*La Heronnière* on the 1612 map—for the heron roosting there. It's possible Champlain spent the evening of September 5, 1604, near Schoodic Island, perhaps sheltering from a southwest wind on the east side of it.

A modest sea explodes on Schoodic Peninsula as the wind-driven gulf leans heavily landward. The rain, a lowering sky, and the running sea give the whole venture a strong conclusion. You can feel in the roughening weather the vigor of this coast and of everything that lives here.

Tired of watching birds but still wanting to take in every moment of the voyage, I can't stop naming their vivid, useful particularity—gulls and eiders and cormorants mostly, a loon here and there floating strangely on the heaving water. But at the end of a long day, what's left to see but the day itself, the leading edge of autumn running strong on the end of summer, time itself running hard in the form of gray, whitened waves and the darkening of the first autumn evening.

Finally, we clear *Cap Enragé*, its black granite whitening loudly.

Therefore investigate mountains thoroughly. When you investigate mountains thoroughly, this is the work of the mountains.

—EIHEI DŌGEN,
"MOUNTAINS AND WATERS SUTRA"

CAIRNS —

Mountains Walking

Autumn moves easily across Mount Desert, an affair of changing light and shorter days. Birch and aspen rustle, salt marshes molt from emerald green to tan. Bursts of wind ruffle ponds and lakes. The turning tide seems to have a snap to it, an insistence, especially on cool, blue evenings when I know I'm going to light a fire in the cabin when I get home.

After two months of summer haze that denies the landscape depth of field, the sky becomes interesting again, full of clouds and change, restless as the water beneath it, or so still and blue it hurts, a backlit dome that highlights the grain in things. The island's bare summits seem large again in the clear air. Hiking, you can hear the flow of the small streams hidden on their slopes.

In autumn on the coast of Maine, no two days are the same.

Every morning from mid-September through late October brings a new season. You move from one field moment to another, randomly absorbing experiences that weave themselves into your memory. Walking down by the Bass Harbor lighthouse, you encounter cedar waxwings in the mountain ash, the slender limbs of which are heavy with long-stemmed clusters of orange fruit. Paddling out of Seal Cove, you find yourself surrounded by odd seabirds, vaguely familiar, that you've never seen before. You realize later, perusing a field guide over a plate of scallops, that these were young-of-the-year black guillemots, this year's birds newly minted. You walk the Ship Harbor Trail listening to the absence of warblers, the gusty silence of birdless woods.

Or out at Schoodic Peninsula one evening, sitting on the rocks while feasting on a grilled-cheese sandwich and a Styrofoam bowl of fish chowder from the takeout in Birch Harbor, you watch a perfect vee of Canada geese turn, disassemble in the air, and land on the quiet water between Big Moose and Little Moose Islands. Softly gabbling, they settle themselves among the grebes and loons. Or photographing Great Meadow at dawn, you watch the way flushing white-tailed deer startle sparrows out of the tall grasses, while that perfect bowl of space between Huguenot Head and Dorr Mountain fills with daylight.

Autumn is, of course, the finest season for walking. Any trail through the island's quiet woods will give you access to the details of a time of year that, unlike spring, is always in motion, never still. The Gorge Path is one way through the heart of autumn. One of the older recreational trails on the island, this path up the dark ravine that forms the rocky crease between Cadillac and Dorr Mountains appears on maps and in guidebooks as early as the 1870s. In a modest way, it's a dramatic path, a walk of a few miles into the heart of Mount Desert, as a realm of woods, that takes you suddenly up onto its bare, open summits, another world entirely.

I like to slip into those woods in late September just after dawn. Along the Park Loop Road, where you find the trailhead, the wind rustles a fringe of burnt-land trees, the deciduous regrowth after the Great Fire of 1947—white birch and red maple, red oak and mountain maple, hobblebush everywhere berried out for the birds. There is a little spruce and beech, some white pine and of course eastern hemlock thick along the stream courses.

The trail rises at the pleasant pitch of the island's lower slopes, the ground beneath my boots rising and falling into the quiet, early autumn woods. I've dressed light for a cool morning, intending to walk myself warm. At times the trail loses itself in the darkness of thick stands of hemlock, out of which I am surprised not to be flushing ruffed grouse or at least hearing the muffled, ground-hugging whir of their wings. Along some stretches, it climbs across small, sunlit granite balds pioneered at the edges by heaths and ferns.

At one point a deer clatters up the slope—heavy on the hoof and therefore a buck, I think—but so well hidden by the vegetation I'll never know. I can sense the weight of the animal in the fading echoes of that startling clatter and, a little farther on, find the gleaming sheen of a buck rub on a red maple, hard evidence of polished antlers.

Eventually the trail finds the empty bed of Kebo Brook, an intermittent stream that drains this narrow watershed. Mount Desert's small streams share the volatile character given to them by the island's topography. Given their short, steep granite watercourses, they are either flowing hard, full of mountainous energy and eager for the sea—like the upper reaches of Otter Creek in a rainy spring—or they lie hidden underground, flowing, if they flow at all, invisibly down the mountains.

In its lower reaches, this streambed is dry and empty, a twenty-foot-wide jumble of rock waiting for water. Crossing it back and forth as the trail wends, you can feel the expectancy, the tension in the space, see the pure shape of a stream in the woods, the idea of it.

A mile or two up the mountain, I ford the dry, empty husk of Kebo Brook within earshot of flowing water, a sound as irresistible as a bird call, as good a murmur as a whirring grouse. I walk up the streambed until I see a spout of water pouring over a mossy lip of granite, as graceful a gesture as a pitcher being poured there between the two mountains. In indigenous terms, this is the visible *person* of the stream, another speaking being in the woods, another aspect of the life of the island revealed by the spareness of autumn.

The stream is coming down the mountain like a living being, which of course it is. I walk up along this threshold of the stream's appearance, a braid of water and rock. Without thinking about it, I avoid stepping on the flowing water. Moss-dark pools brim upstream of where I stand. If I listen intently, I can hear a quiet cacophony at my feet. A small pond of clear, cold water disappears under itself where the stream is working to fill its bed for the next overflow down the mountain—as good an image of the living edge of autumn as you could ask to encounter.

I note a gnarly, double-trunked red maple at this spot, a twisted, broken-branched old thing that is still putting a few leaves into the canopy, photosynthesizing energy into matter, connecting the sun to the stream near which it is rooted and into which it will shed its leaves.

From this point, the quiet sound of flowing water organizes the woods. The morning is not much for birds, but I hear the abrupt, distinct cackle of a red-bellied woodpecker on the slopes and, a little farther on, the rising mockery of a pileated woodpecker. At one point, I pass ranks of gray birch trying to hold what's left of summer in this forest, now that daylight has gotten into the watershed. The birch leaves are green but beginning to pale. You can feel the coolness in the air and hear the rustling of the canopy overhead and you know that autumn has taken hold and is slowly showing its hand. Here and there, a red maple has turned bright red.

The trail rises steeply up the stream course into the gorge for which the path is named, the north side of the eroded saddle between Dorr and Cadillac Mountains, taking you along dark, wet cliffs hung with lichens, mosses, and ferns. There is a flat-topped rock formation, maybe thirty feet tall, that looks like a sea stack left in the woods. This must be what is designated Pulpit Rock on early trail maps, but the quaint name has fallen into disuse and the dark stack of granite stands for itself now, stone eroding as it will, not intending to be picturesque, a natural not a human thing.

In places, the stream and the path are nearly the same, the latter a mossy, wet shoulder-wide cascade of stone steps in which one can see the efforts, shuffled by time and weather, of century-old trail building. In places it's hard to decipher which parts of the trail are natural and which are the work of human hands—a supreme compliment to the labor here. Park literature indicates plans to rebuild and improve these old trails, but I think many of them, including the Gorge Path, have devolved into a perfect state of dishevelment, a good compromise between human intentions and natural processes.

This gorge is not spectacular in a western sense, nothing on Mount Desert is. Walking slowly, you are through it in an hour. But it is a perfect example of the rugged, bucolic places hidden all over Mount Desert Island—the source of its soulfulness. Visually, the quiet beauty of the island's forested interior is Romantic, in the nineteenth-century sense. John Muir might be dissatisfied walking up the Gorge Path, finding no cataclysmic glamour, no soul-stirring danger in it, but the young William Wordsworth would be at home clambering up its wet rocks through its hemlocks and yellow birch. What for some of us is the reassuring, relatively undisturbed natural life of Mount Desert's quiet places corresponds to a nineteenth-century idea of the rustic wild—"the tall rock / The mountain, and the deep and gloomy wood," landscapes scaled to a day's walk and a day's thought, nearby places that offer a profound change of scene.

An enormous eastern hemlock—perhaps the finest of that great species in the park—grows high up in the gorge, I think where the path crosses Kebo Brook for the last time. Taking my outstretched arms as a rough-and-ready fathom, this fine tree is nearly two fathoms in circumference. The tree looks as sound as a ship mast, a massive column of wood and living tissue, thirty or forty feet of clear bole to its first limb and taller than I can estimate.

White pine, not hemlock, was the tree for ship masts, but this hemlock helps take the imagination back to those forests of 220-foot-tall white pine, which did in fact become the main masts of the British and American navies. This fine hemlock holds a place in the canopy surrounded by yellow birch, a hardy, ragged-looking species that occupies these upper slopes and manages to force its way out of an unpromising seedbed of slowly weathering scree.

The trail follows the narrow way between the dense pinch of contour lines you see on a topographic map, where Dorr and Cadillac look like adjacent fingerprints. The western side of Dorr Mountain is a dark cliff of impressive stonework, a textbook illustration of ice-fractured granite, a museum of every kind of spall. The fracturing of the exposure makes Dorr look like it was built out of rectangular blocks of granite, a great work of masonry. Superficial caves are forming here and there, creating all sorts of niches and microniches for plant and insect life that only a trained biologist could parse. Tucked away from marine and oceanic influences, you see terrestrial energies at work stirring pioneering vegetation out of bedrock, creating soil with the erosive power of tiny roots of mosses and ferns, sending the roots of seedlings into fissures, eventually bursting bedrock with the roots of full-grown trees.

The trunks of dead, two-foot-thick spruce and pine lay hung up on the face of the cliff, windfalls that have outlived their purchase on the rock. The cliff hosts every moisture and shade-loving lichen, fern, shrub, and tree that has made its way into this watershed. Great yellow birch, festooned with thick, waxy shelves of polyphores, grow in the shadows where there are more rotting snags than living trees. This is a strong place, in an indigenous sense, a violent place over time—given the jumble of boulders all around me and the great trees hung up in midfall—but peaceful in the moment. That contrast is what people have been walking up here for centuries to experience. That is what Pulpit Rock is preaching: this is the way nature works.

I meet the sun coming up over the eastern edge of the gorge, my dark morning walk to the bright summit world coinciding with its arc over the island. By now that sunlight will be warming Mount Desert's granite domes, creating the thermals that migrating raptors seek as they come across Frenchman Bay from the mainland. I pass smaller, fern-shrouded cliffs dripping water into small streams, each contributing a little momentum to the quiet head of Kebo Brook as it makes its way, pool by pool, down the gorge.

Up on the cobble of the saddle between Dorr and Cadillac, the tree life thins to a fine array of yellow birch, white birch, mountain maple, and, finally, a mountain ash, a tree I admired for years as a summit-wanderer in the southern Appalachians, where it grows on rock outcrops at the highest elevations, its bloom and fruit good company in spring and fall. Here the ash in places grows at the water's edge, though it will also take hold in the highlands, where it feeds warblers and other passerines on their migration south.

Near the ash, I catch a glimpse of Frenchman Bay over the shoulder of Dorr. I start hearing the *chips* of juncos, the *pips* of yellow-throats, and the rustle of that northeasterly breeze that brings migrating raptors over the bay. Mount Desert is a generous landscape; to walk here is to move from one gift to another. Suddenly the day is warm, more summerlike than autumnal. Having enjoyed the dark woods, I am equally glad of the light and space and the chance to take a longer view of things.

This trail crossing is familiar from many hikes over the years. If you cultivate an interest in Mount Desert's modest backcountry, you will cross your own track many times, pass by the same weathered wooden trail signs in many seasons and from different directions. I come through this way in summer from the south on a walk over Dorr Mountain and in the spring as part of a long circuit up the east face of Dorr, over Cadillac, the way I am going today, and then down the south ridge of Cadillac to follow Canon Brook back to The Tarn. There are all sorts of ways of weaving yourself into this landscape, of putting yourself in the way of things.

Today I scramble up the east side of Cadillac, feeling the steep pitch of each bulge of the slope in my calves and thighs and stomach. I move from cairn to cairn—traditional stone markers of *the way* here—staying on a path that tries to minimize disturbance to fragile summit vegetation. Going up the long rise, you have to turn and look frequently, admiring, for reasons difficult to articulate, views you have seen from other angles—the mainland, Frenchman Bay, Schoodic Peninsula, the Gulf of Maine. You see the shape and structure of Dorr Mountain, the fragmented bulk of it, the simple weight and strength of granite molded into a mountain, the strong arc of it juxtaposed to the joint failures of its eroding face. You see, graphically, how the strength and weakness of a mountain is one and the same and how mountains, which move slowly through time, have a life of their own.

The gulf shines like silk, a pointillistic display of light, nothing of water to be seen, really, except its reflectiveness to the noonday sun. I take in the familiar display of peninsulas and islands, the world of pleasing fragments arrayed around Mount Desert, the canny shapes of all this islanded land. As I walk toward higher vantage, Baker Island and the Cranberry Isles and the Duck Islands come into view, all set in that amazing shimmer of watery light, an impossible glare—no boats or buoys visible, just the brilliant sheen of the Gulf of Maine on a cool, sunlit day in early autumn.

The *thing itself* you think you sometimes see from these slopes—not life, *bios*, but whatever it is makes life possible, the *scene* of it—that is what you can see from here, as I do today standing on the western slopes of Cadillac. I am well below the summit hubbub, surrounded by groves of mountain ash hung with clusters of near-ripe pomes and stunted birch turning yellow in the season, losing leaves to the same breeze that brings hawks to the thermals rising from the sun-warmed granite at my feet. Perhaps it's just fatigue or exhilaration, or a perfect ratio of the two, but some days, when hiking the summits, Mount Desert Island seems like fuel for a fabulous fire. Or perhaps Mount Desert itself is a cairn, as are its outer islands. Perhaps they all mark a trail, a *way*. Small spruce and thick-branched heaths shudder in that wind, everything tuned to the rough thrum of the season.

I bird the cover, walking slowly up toward what I know is a disenchanting summit, that hawk wind sometimes pressing hard at my back and keeping most of the warblers well hidden, picking berries in the impenetrable shadows of the heaths. The play of sunlight and wind in the stunted summit trees is itself something to see, an agitation out of which a bird flits occasionally before disappearing behind jittering birch leaves or the thick windscreen of spruce boughs—sparrows, warblers, chickadees, juncos. At one point I catch the zing of a kestrel twisting the air overhead in some impossible bank, distracting me just as the impression of a hummingbird stitches its way by me. A raven tilts on the warm air, cavorting, shallow-diving, practicing its powers on the wind. Around me, the graceful swords of ash leaves are in every stage of turning dark wine red.

At the top, I skirt the busy parking lot, an unavoidable

disappointment, and set myself down for lunch at the hawk-watch site on the north shoulder of Cadillac. Every year, the Park Service conducts a daily count of migrating raptors from early September to late October. A ranger or two and a handful of volunteers can be found in all but the worst weather watching the skies to the east and north for the dark forms of birds coming across Frenchman Bay.

Broad-winged hawks are passing in good numbers today, soaring high overhead, easing their way toward South America and the Amazon Basin. The closer you look, the more you see, dozens of birds in some thermals, easing east. When sunlight catches them underneath, you can see the distinctive black-and-white banding of their tails.

Once you learn the knack of scanning what seem at first to be empty skies, you begin to pick up the distant forms of what turn out to be eagles and osprey, the familiar turkey vulture and rare peregrines, as well as other hawks and falcons that proceed along the coast every autumn. The volunteers call birds with pleasing frequency—an osprey way out over Schoodic, a bald eagle coming across The Narrows, what must be broad-wings kettling over the mainland, northern goshawks and rough-legged hawks, harriers and red-tailed and red-shouldered hawks, kestrels coming on fast and low or coming up suddenly on drafts up the sides of Dorr, sharp-shins streaking by. Tribes of birds that have bred and nested, reared young and eaten their fill as tundra and taiga hunters, or as marsh birds or coastal birds, are moving out of their summer grounds in the low Arctic and sub-Arctic toward their wintering quarters. In passing, they will cast their fleeting shadows over farm fields and towns, backyards and cities.

This great migration of raptors reminds you how well birds

have adapted to use the earth, how successful their natural histories are, and how vulnerable are their far-ranging needs. At a pinch point like this one, where so many species are funneled together—all seeking the advantage of rock-warmed air rising under their wings—migration seems to be a communal instinct, a collective harvesting of the year's last warm days.

There are monarch butterflies migrating also, wingbeat by wingbeat toward Mexico, and hummingbirds returning to the tropics from their foray in the brief, boreal summer. Raptors are wonderfully concentrated here and juxtaposed in instructive ways. We get to see a kestrel and a merlin careening near each other for comparison. An occasional Cooper's hawk shows the way its rounded tail is distinct from the sharp-shin's. The sharpies are swift, graceful fliers, inclined to fold themselves and dive on the wind, stooping with the aerodynamic sleekness of peregrines. The kestrels tend frequently to stall and hover—wings fanned wide and tails spread—until the chance arises to drop down on a meal of dragonfly or other prey. In migration, they are an aggressive, beautifully agitated bird, not the patient creature I see perched on phone lines along the cornfields in Pennsylvania.

After lunch and some conversation and a check of the tally of the season's birds, I leave my post on the fringe of the hawk watch and head slowly down Cadillac's North Ridge Trail. A few hundred feet below the summit, I get a fine view of an immature bald eagle rising on a thermal. At first I thought it was a turkey vulture, but its broad, outstretched wings were flat as a board. And, even at a distance, it was too large to be anything other than an eagle. This young bird is speckled black and white underneath and has dark tail feathers and only a bit of white on its gray head.

I walk on but have to stop again, this time to watch a palm warbler feeding in the heaths.

In the end, I'm just walking, taking in the landscape as it flows by me. This is what the thirteenth-century Zen master Dōgen suggests, to walk in the mountains until the mountains begin to walk through you, to move respectfully, hoping to earn respect, to bow toward everything. In long, easy strides I give up the altitude I gained, step by step, coming up the gorge this morning. I can see the dark crease of forest up through which I passed. Sargent Mountain, to the west, looks inviting for more autumn hiking, more mountains walking. I will, in fact, haunt its broad slopes for a week and then, as if I have an obligation, move on to the short, steep trails around St. Sauveur and Acadia Mountains, across Somes Sound. Finally, I will let all the good, quiet woods around Western Mountain walk through me also. I'll sit on those broad granite ledges overlooking Bartlett Narrows and Blue Hill Bay and watch autumn harden into fall.

Today, I move between granite balds and stunted woods, wind rustling oak and birch and silencing itself into spruce and fir. Chickadees, juncos, titmice, and yellow-rumps insist on the ordinariness of summit life. Something is going purple on the lower slopes and something else is going orange. In the end this walking melts into impressions. By the time I stop to admire the fine views of Eagle Lake from the North Ridge Trail, I feel as if I am in a painting looking at another painting, lost in the artful nature of the mountains here.

*And in this way he made Man: He
took his bow and arrows and
shot at trees, the basket trees, the Ash.
Then the Indians came out of the bark of
the Ash-trees.*

—PASSAMAQUODDY LEGEND

TOWARD *PEMETIC*—

Spirit of Place

Rainy days on Mount Desert are excellent for hiking and for
coast-watching—you could do worse than sit among spruce in
fog—but when all your foul-weather gear is soaked from too
many successive wet days, you might let your steps slap through
the doorway of the Abbe Museum in Bar Harbor.

All during 2006, the Abbe's visiting exhibit room was graced
with the artwork of Abenaki children.* This display consisted of
drawings, charcoals, pastels, paintings, woodcuts, a lithograph,

---

* Partly due to cultural misunderstanding and partly due to changing linguistic and scholarly
conventions, the English spelling of tribal names continues to shift. *Abenaki* has long been used
to refer to the Eastern Algonquin, although *Wabanaki* has also come into use. For consistency,
I have used the former—the preference in *Webster's Third Edition*—throughout this book. But
note that *Waponahki* is now preferred by some Passamaquoddy, as is evidenced by the title of
this art show.

and a photograph as well as two object-images—one of clay and wood, the other of plaster.

The art of schoolchildren too often is briefly admired in order to be dismissed. Artwork hangs in the classrooms and hallways of every school everywhere, one step away from the refrigerator door. These images hung in the Abbe Museum for a long time—all year, I think—starkly displayed on the bare walls of a well-lit, high-ceilinged room, Abenaki music quietly drifting in the air.

I have to admit that I may have ignored the room on my first visit or, like others, walked through it quickly, inattentively, to see if there was anything on display worth my time, an adult courtesy to the naiveté of schoolchildren. Although drawn at first to archaeological displays, which I already knew how to admire, I came to spend more and more time with the "2006 Waponahki Student Art Show," sometimes stopping in at the museum just to reobserve a particular image—*Swimming Bear* or *Fire Dancing*, *Putep*, or *Dragonflies*—and sometimes to enjoy the bright, tribal energy of the collection as a whole. These visits came to be as good as going to the woods, as high a compliment as I can make. The only thing I lacked was a log or a stump on which to sit.

Of course, there is an art to visiting a museum, just as there is an art to walking in the woods or shuffling along the shelf rock of the tidal zone. Museums have the challenging task of formally presenting the genius of life—the conscious expressions of sub-conscious intuitions in art and, especially in the Abbe's case, in artifacts, humble objects of cultural subsistence like arrowheads and scrapers, hammerstones and bone flutes, beadwork and bas-ketry. Presenting the frank art of schoolchildren was even more difficult, since such displays can easily cloy and satisfy only something sentimental in us. The spare, stark way this work of young Passamaquoddy was presented made it clear that the exhibit was not a sentimental gesture. The wise sponsors of this show understood what they had on hand in these images, and they thoughtfully left them on display for a long time for visitors to discover.

I was on Mount Desert a good part of 2006 and visited the Abbe frequently, not always waiting for the excuse of a rainy day. That happened also to be a year when I was reading what I could find of Abenaki mythology—stories from *N'karnayoo*, "the long ago time when people lived always in the early red morning, before sunrise." I had a particular interest in the way the coastal landscape and its wildlife and birds were used in ancient storytelling.

I have written about the Cherokee and the way their language and tribal imagination were shaped by the Southern Appalachians, and I teach a university seminar on Deep Ecology and Native American Storytelling. As a writer, I have long understood that part of understanding any landscape is understanding the stories it inspired, the ways in which land, weather, vegetation, and wildlife influence the nature of its oldest narratives. Indeed, the vocabulary and grammar of Native American languages have been deeply influenced by what Thoreau called the "tawny grammar" of nature itself. As I spent time with the exhibit, I learned to see the art of Abenaki schoolchildren both as a strong expression of individual vision and as part of a collective intuition of deep ecology by young Passamaquoddy.

Most obvious in this work was a love of and respect for animals. A moose was admired for its size and strength (the works were accompanied by brief artist statements). Joy was taken in the rabbit—*Matawehso*—a trickster figure in Abenaki and Micmac lore. A fox family was depicted following a river up into the mountains. A whale swam through "an ocean of colors," a beautiful depiction of what might be a whale's consciousness of the diffraction and diffusion of light in layers of water and sky. There were the face of an eagle and an otter, both drawn because they were "beautiful" and "important," and a "feasting wolf" with the blood-red muzzle of a natural predator. There were exotic pronghorn antelope, drawn because the artist had heard they were endangered. There were horses and a perched eagle and also dragonflies, the latter a colorful acknowledgment of the importance of insects in the tales and creation myths of many Native American people.

Modern cultures restrict personhood to human beings, a selfish and dangerous contraction of awareness and sympathy. Primal cultures distribute personhood throughout nature. In such societies, animals and plants, even mountains and rivers, are spoken of as being *people*—beings with status equal to the status of human beings. Everything in nature has sentience and purpose. All beings, animate and inanimate, have gifts and powers. The mythic truth of such perceptions is perfectly compatible with the facts of natural history and of deep ecology as we are now coming to understand them. Myth and science are both necessary to appreciate the wisdom of the living earth and the personhood of all living things. Passamaquoddy children understand this. "*N'kah-ne-noo*. In old times, in the beginning of things, men were as animals and animals as men; how this was, no one knows."

Among the most marvelous of the images was Kelsey Anne

Shepard's *Swimming Bear.* The artist explains what I cannot describe: "This is a picture of a bear swimming by the colorful islands. The night sky has the northern lights. The waves are strong and the bear is trying to go through them. I chose a bear because it's my Passamaquoddy name, Muwin. I made the bear colorful because she is different from them all."

Ms. Shepard's collage is strong art. She depicts the natural world as vivid with form and force—jagged pink islands, dark blue waves, a sky full of unresolved energies. At the center, where we would expect to see something important happening, we find an equally vivid depiction of the being of her familiar spirit struggling heroically through the way that nature is—supportive but resistant. The bear holds its head up uncomplainingly, meeting the strength of the waves with the strength of its swimming, carrying its colors through a colorful world. As the artist notes, the bear is unique, but it is also a mythic bear, the form of all bears, a recognition that in nature all beings are different and the same, that all *persons*— children, islands, bears—are different and the same. The collage has more to say, but I believe that is the heart of it. Not bad for a third-grader to convey. Not bad for an adult to finally see.

We learn in Abenaki legends, principally Micmac and Passamaquoddy, that any granite island might be a sacred canoe in disguise. The demigod Glooskap—the Master of animals and plants who created human beings and who helped fashion the world as we know it—kept his canoe hidden in this way, anticipating various journeys and chores, anywhere from Nova Scotia's Minas Basin to the mouth of Maine's Saco River. In the primal mind, there is no sharp division between natural and cultural objects; in the mythic world, there has been no tragic split between nature and human nature.

Glooskap's canoe might be anywhere—islands are not always what they seem. (The so-called Porcupine Islands are, for example, the bones of a moose.) Islands might be more colorful, in spirit, than they appear. In one tale, needing to go on a journey, Glooskap points "to a small island of granite which rose amid the waves, and it was covered with tall pine-trees. 'There is my canoe!' said he; and when he had taken them unto it, it became a real canoe." As Kelsey Anne Shepard's colorful collage suggests, an island might be many things, all sorts of visionary truths might be hidden in one's native landscape. The coast of Maine and the Canadian Maritimes are rich with mythic granite and transformative fogs. Ask any fisherman. "Over all the Land of the Wabanaki there is no place which was not marked by the hand of the Master."

One September evening I was paddling a canoe up Marshall Brook, at the head of Bass Harbor Marsh. Near sunset I rode a high tide into the lower brook, where it bends into the sinuous periodicity of some meander dictated by the physics of its flow and the distribution of its sediments. The tide bulged into low marsh. I paddled quietly, as though I belonged there, enjoying the way the world seemed poised between water and light, everything solid, myself included, a conspiracy of those two elements.

Light reflected off the purple wing patches of male mallards flushing wildly. Light disappeared into the greasy gloss of sodden cormorants slapping their way off the water. Light lit the stout form of a kingfisher doing maneuvers in the air that might impress a kestrel, the kingfisher retreating upmarsh carrying its territorial protests ahead of my intrusion.

I enjoyed, as I always did, paddling toward the bulk of Western Mountain, its notched form a fine indigenous design. The mountain was still green with summer, but autumn was rustling in the air around me, and the oncoming season seemed reified in the restlessness of waterfowl and the absence of songbirds, flycatchers and warblers no longer showing themselves in numbers. A headwind from the north gave me something to dig into and in places vaned the canoe perfectly between the narrowing banks of the marsh. The island and its mountains turned as the creek turned—space is indeed as curved as physicists insist. At one point I could see Beech Mountain and its fire tower, a good site in September for watching raptors that I knew must be moving overhead or, in summer, for sleeping in the sun.

One stirs oneself along in a marsh, studying for that narrow ribbon of deep water where a tide-drowned creek is hidden. In places I could dig deep into the tannic water, enjoying a wide grasp to the throat of the paddle and a full pull with the blade. In others I could only make sweeping dabs in shallows where marsh grasses hissed on the hull. Kneeling in the canoe, shoulders square to the bank, I had a perfect view of where I was.

Two cormorant dried themselves on a spruce snag, the ancient-looking birds and the dry, gray wood looking equally timeless, a joined image of some patient watchfulness in nature that would never change. A slight disturbance in the water became the gray head of an otter, which soon twitched into the flurry of a shallow dive creased with a slick, arched back and the hint of a tail. The otter came up on the far bank with a fair-size fish in its mouth

and then disappeared up a trail of beaten grass. As I was noticing some yellow wildflowers along the marsh edge, a great blue
heron, flushed from a tree, squawking inelegantly.

The kingfisher kept moving on ahead of me, mallards quacked
away, a chickadee bulleted into a tamarack. I watched for wood
ducks—Thoreau's *summer ducks*—but they were gone. The marsh
itself had gone to seed, grasses nodding with the weight of summer's
wild grain. Warm days go quickly cool in September, and as the
day wanes, if you watch closely enough, you can see the afternoon
simmering of a marsh suddenly stiffen into a chill evening. The few
large dragonflies seemed out of season and I could feel the absence
of songbirds and sense the unseen hustle of departure everywhere.

We see what we are prepared to see, both those things that we
have put ourselves in the way of encountering—we go out looking for wolves or whales—and those things that finally reveal
themselves to us—cedar waxwings in a pitch pine, the colors of a
tidal pool. Nature encourages us to think and feel in primal ways,
to clear our heads and hearts of noise, to observe the found world
closely, partly to see it for what it is and partly to absorb it as a
threshold for imaginative understanding of the nature of nature
and our place therein.

As the sun began to set, sending long, low-angled shafts of
light into the marsh, I noticed the tide gently sliding seaward.
Algae and other flotsam shifted with the changed flow. Reluctant
to let the hour go, I paddled on a bit farther.

I moved slowly upcreek, hoping the last wood ducks of the season would flush from the edge of the grasses and send me back on
my way. Instead of wood ducks, however, I was given the tops of
some tall grasses moving oddly, seedheads jerking out of tune with

the evening breeze—just at the bank thirty yards ahead of me on the right. *Something* there. I watched for minutes, eventually easing the canoe forward small stroke by small stroke until I could hear the extraordinary sound of grasses being torn in browse. I guessed what was hidden there but could not see it, even from fifteen yards away. But I could vividly see an insistent appetite in the way the tall grasses jerked about. I could hear hunger in the marsh that evening as life fed toward the edge of the silty creek that was draining back toward Bass Harbor under my hull.

I knelt there in the canoe, keeping still, proud and ramrod straight, the paddle in front of me across the thwarts—as if this was the proper, formal pose for such watching. Finally, as beautiful a sculpting of antlers as I have ever seen rose into the golden evening light. Not a large rack, in the parlance of trophy hunters, but a fine eight-pointer, at once a perfect image and a perfect embodiment of a white-tailed deer coming into regenerative maturity in the hospitable recesses of a salt marsh.

The beam and tines were dark brown, probably only recently out of velvet, and they flashed a tawny yellow in the sunlight, holding that sunlight as if the antlers were a strangely figured bowl, an expression of energy that gathered energy, another seedhead in the marsh. I can picture it still, rooted there in the sunlight at the muddy edge of Marshall Brook. The deer looked as though it had come up for air.

Mount Desert Island is a good place to practice being indigenous. I think that is all I want to say and why I keep coming back and why I spend a lot of time in places I have been before. At every turn, Mount Desert invites you to slowly become native to this coast, to its nature, its wildlife and plant life, its weather and seasons.

According to the Passamaquoddy, human beings came forth from black ash trees:

> Glooskap came first of all into this country, into Nova Scotia, Maine, Canada, into the land of the Wabanaki, next to sunrise. There were no Indians here then (only wild Indians very far to the west).
>
> First born were the Mikumwess, the Oonahgemessuk, the small Elves, little men, dwellers in rocks.
>
> And in this way he made Man: He took his bow and arrows and shot at trees, the basket-trees, the Ash. Then Indians came out of the bark of the Ash-trees. . . .

Native American creation myths confirm—often in beautiful, unexpected ways—the intimacy of nature and human nature. The soulfulness of human life does not come down from the sky—it comes from the earth or from the sea or from rivers or out of the woods. This is not folklore, this business of human beings stepping forth from black ash summoned by the impact and quiver of Glooskap's cedar arrows. If you let your own consciousness be worn down by the subtle ways of this landscape, you will begin to see the indigenous truth of this place, its unfathomable soul, a soul well hidden underneath its tourist trappings but there nonetheless on any morning or evening, on any day in any weather.

Become indigenous here and you will understand what young Passamaquoddy artists understand, that the voices of loons were a gift of the gods, that this tribe of birds was blessed with transcendental speech. You will not be surprised to learn that the Abenaki have been singing to whales for thousands of years, that long before sonar confirmed the fact, they understood that song was this great animal's preferred mode of speech. In Micmac legends, whales sing when they are stranded, and Glooskap saves them, in turn, with song: "Have no fear, *noogume*, / You shall not suffer, / You shall swim in the sea once more."

Indigenous hours wait here for the taking. Landscape and weather and random forays can easily lead you to interesting thresholds of consciousness. Spend a rainy hour taking shelter in a sea cave stranded in the woods. Study crows in wet pines. Wander among the glacial erratics arranged like sculpture on the southern ridge of Penobscot Mountain. Study the sky and the way the calls of warblers fill the large space around you. Sit alongside the wetland on Pemetic Mountain comparing the trilling of juncos to that of yellow-rumped warblers. Paddle the quiet eastern shore of Seal Cove Pond. Leave your canoe at the mouth of a brook and walk up into the woods. Sit down. Bird the tall spruce at Pretty Marsh from a kayak at sunset, when the trees are lit with long rays of receding daylight. If the evening is still, paddle the glass water to Folly Island counting coup on loons and harbor seals. Walk the wrack line anywhere. Sift through tidal pools. Watch the sky. Study water. Give in to the uncanny impression that you are home and not at home in this landscape, that you are one with this place and other to it, that you belong here—like a deer feeding in a marsh—and that you are foreign, an intruder—a man in a canoe. Imagine, finally, some day walking the burnt-land woods in the rain or sleeping on a rock ledge up on Western Mountain, or staring mesmerized as a tidal pool fills, that you are a black ash tree with an arrow vibrating in your heartwood about to step forward into the life of the world.

*onsider them both, the sea and
the land; and do you not find a strange
analogy to something in yourself?*

—HERMAN MELVILLE,
MOBY-DICK

LAST LIGHT—

Mount Desert Rock

We travel to islands to be partly at sea.

I'm watching the worn summits of Mount Desert Island in the moonlight from Mount Desert Rock, twenty-six miles offshore. A cool southwesterly stirs calm water, ruffling a dark sheen of small waves. The Gulf of Maine wraps broadly around the horizon under a dome of sky unbelievably bright with stars. A lighthouse swings its beam dutifully and sounds a foghorn, unnecessary tonight, every thirty seconds. On the northeast side of the island, beyond a weathered boathouse, dozens of gray and harbor seals glisten darkly, lounging on exposed ledges where the tide rustles in the rockweed and slaps at the irregular edges of this durable speck of land.

Occasionally, and for no apparent reason, hundreds of greater black-backed gulls get up en masse, rustling into the air, and begin a clockwise circling of Mount Desert Rock. This mesmerizing exercise seems ritualistic rather than natural. Sometimes I remember it at an odd moment at home, thinking that the scene is from a Greek play or something in Yeats. Occasionally I dream of these gulls whirling about the island as if Mount Desert Rock were the center of something, the flock of black-backs turning hard because the birds insist on flying so fast around so small a space. What is centripetal and centrifugal in this ritual seems to cancel out. Either the island holds the flock together or the birds keep the island in place. In dreams, and I think in reality, the gulls are silent except for the commotion of their wings above the wash of the tide, the keening of the seals, and the Celtic mourn of the foghorn.

From Mount Desert Rock, Mount Desert Island has just begun to sink below the horizon. It fits Samuel de Champlain's description of it as having "the appearance to one at sea, as of seven or eight mountains extending along near each other," but those mountains are on the verge of becoming islands. Champlain Mountain and Huguenot Head already look separated by water from the broad expanse of Dorr and Cadillac Mountains. From a little farther out, Pemetic, Sargent, and Norumbega Mountains would each seem to occupy its own island. West of Somes Sound, Mount Desert would break up into three islands separated by the glacial grooves of Long Pond and Echo Lake.

To see Mount Desert Island from Mount Desert Rock is to discover it in reverse, to go back in time and recloak it in topographic uncertainty, recover it as unknown. Despite all the changes wrought by technology, the curvature of the earth remains what it is. At a certain distance—fifteen or twenty miles—landmarks begin to disappear. Approach Mount Desert from the sea for the first time, not knowing it is there, and you would watch seven or eight islands rise and fuse into a single island—a strange and beautiful landform unlike any other on the east coast of North America.

From Mount Desert Rock, you have nearly the same vantage John Winthrop had when he sketched Mount Desert Island from the deck of the *Arbella* on the eighth of June in 1630, sixteen years after Champlain's first coasting. The *Arbella* had cleared Cornwall on the tenth of April and weathered her share of storms on her North Atlantic crossing, making the Grand Banks on the twenty-third of May and landfall off Cape Sable, Nova Scotia, on the sixth of June, the fifty-ninth day of her voyage. By midafternoon of June 8, after making slow headway against a stiff southwest wind, Winthrop recounts an auspicious if unexpected landfall:

> The winde still w: & by S: faire weather, but close & colde. We stood n:n:w: with a stiffe gale, & about 3: in the afternoone we had sight of lande to the n: w: about 15 le[agues]: which we supposed was the Iles of monthegen [Monhegan Island] but it proved mounte mansell [Mount Desert Island]. Then we tacked and stood w:S:w: we had nowe faire sunneshine weather, & so pleasant a sweet ethere, as did muche refreshe vs [us], & there came a smell off the shore like the smell of a garden.
>
> There came a wilde pigeon into our shippe & another smalle lande birde.

The *Arbella* was hoping to make the coast of Maine farther west than what the English—rejecting French names and claims—called Mount Mansell, but Champlain's *Isle des Monts Déserts* was an unmistakable geographic landmark then poised uncertainly on the contested border between New England and New France. Winthrop sketched Mount Desert carefully, for reference, as he did other coastal features between this landfall and Cape Ann. His drawing shows the major peaks and hints at the U-shaped glacial cirques between them. His pen strokes—preserved on a stained, ragged page of his journal—flow confidently along the contours of the island's distinctive shape, a close gathering of mountains that cannot be confused with any other place. Given the completeness of detail along the shoreline of the island—a careful joining of the lower slopes not quite visible from Mount Desert Rock—the *Arbella* likely was a little closer than Mount Desert Rock when Winthrop made his sketch.

Mount Desert is the most prominent landmark on the northeast coast of North America, and many a seventeenth- and eighteenth-century immigrant coming under sail across the Atlantic on the forty-fifth parallel must have had sight of it, and likely kept a memory of it, on their way to a new life in a new place. America's first great poet, Anne Bradstreet, was on the *Arbella* and undoubtedly was on deck to watch Mount Desert rise up out of the sea and assemble itself as an island. I've gleaned her poems and letters for some reference to it or, more likely, some use of an image inspired by it, but found no trace. Given the risks she faced in the New World—especially as a woman who would bear children on a frontier—and how distressing the distance was between her and her friends and family, it is not likely she saw the soft blue mountains of Mount Desert as beautiful. It is not just the curvature of the earth that changes perceptions.

For centuries, Mount Desert Rock was either a useful landmark or a hazard, depending on the weather. The coastal historian Charles McLane notes that it apparently went unnamed in the seventeenth century and then was charted as Mount Desert Dry Rock in the early eighteenth. From 1830 until 1977, there was a manned lighthouse on the Rock. At first one and then two keepers and their families tended the light and, after 1866, its fog-warning devices. They also somehow tended their extraordinary lives on the most remote light station on the coast of Maine. When just a few years ago, the last children to grow up on the island visited it, they had fond memories of their lives offshore. Thomas Doughty painted the island and its original lighthouse in 1836—as *Desert Rock Lighthouse, Maine*—and again in 1847. He depicted the island well enough, if a little dramatically, but he took the strange liberty of moving it to the mouth of Frenchman Bay, in order to show Mount Desert Island in the background, thereby eliminating the remoteness that makes Mount Desert Rock so distinctive.

The art of keeping a lighthouse standing on Mount Desert Rock apparently had to be learned over time. McLane recounts that the original tower—presumably something very like what Doughty depicted—had to be strengthened only seven years after it was built, rebuilt ten years after that, and refitted nine years later. The current lighthouse is a thick, round tower of granite blocks nearly as sturdy as the island itself. Judging from photographs, the current structure dates back at least to the 1880s. The light and the foghorn were automated in 1977, when the charm and rigor of human lighthouse-keeping came to an end on Mount Desert Rock.

Ownership of the island has passed to the capable stewardship of the College of the Atlantic (COA), but the U.S. Coast Guard continues to own and operate the lighthouse, the foghorn, and a solar-powered weather station on the Rock. Founded in the 1970s with idealistic environmental leanings, COA requires all its students to take a degree in human ecology with a strong emphasis on the challenges of global sustainability. The College of the Atlantic prides itself on the choice of preposition in its name—it is *of* not merely *on* the Atlantic. None of COA's educational resources prove this boast to be *of* the Atlantic as well as does Mount Desert Rock, which is used for a variety of educational purposes, including groundbreaking research conducted by Allied Whale in the Gulf of Maine. The island itself was once a productive whale-watch station, but due to a decline in or a shift of prey species away from adjacent waters, humpbacks, fins, minkes, and other whales don't feed around the island in the numbers they once did.

Mount Desert Rock is close to being the limiting case of an island, or perhaps the Platonic form of an island, or—better—the Stoic ideal of one: a few flat, oblong acres of granite, tapered like a hull from southwest to northeast and, except for the distant company of Mount Desert and a faint view of Long Island and Isle au Haut to the northwest, the Rock is out on its own surrounded by a stunning volume of water that it takes time for a landlubber to get used to. When the Zodiac boat that drops you off on the Rock skids away to the vessel that brought you out, and then that vessel starts slogging back toward Mount Desert, you will have as keen a feeling of being left behind as you can get in these parts.

From the air, Mount Desert Rock looks like the perfect stage

for a production of *The Tempest*,* not because it reminds one of
Prospero's island—which seems more lush and habitable—but
because it embodies the bare grandeur of Shakespeare's mature
art. Sophocles, too, would play well on the Rock. And Beckett.
Nearly soilless, the island is sparsely vegetated with a few grasses
and shrubs, the seeds for which must have migrated with birds or
stowed away on boats and gear and boots. Nothing protects the
Rock from wind and waves except its featurelessness. Its genius
is to lie low. The island's pale gray bedrock—a beautiful, neutral
shade of stone—shelves up to a height of seventeen feet above
sea level. You can do the math for twenty-foot seas. In no posi-
tion to put up any resistance, the Rock ships its share of water in
heavy weather, but when storms clear and seas subside, there it is,
durable as an eider.

Mount Desert Rock is situated between the Inner and Outer
Schoodic Ridges—prominent topographic features on the floor
of the Gulf of Maine that create currents and upwellings that
enrich its marine life. The waters of the continental shelf deepen
quickly around the island, especially seaward, where the sea floor
drops down to 600 and 700 feet below the surface. When you are
on the Rock, you are, in effect, at sea, and the names for things
are underwater. Clay Bank lies to the west and Bank Comfort
to the south-southeast, the Jordan Basin farther out. Beyond the
Jordan Basin, you'll get to the northeast edge of Georges Bank,
beyond which suddenly there would be thousands of feet of water

---

* I am thinking of the wonderful photograph of Mount Desert Rock on page 101 of *Volume II:
Mount Desert to Machias Bay* of Charles B. McLane's *Islands of the Mid-Maine Coast* (Falmouth,
ME: Kennebec River Press, 1989).

under your keel. Mount Desert Rock is the last dry land between the coast of Maine and the Atlantic. And, I'm told, if you sight along the right bearing to the southeast, toward the eastern South Atlantic and the southwest coast of Africa, you are looking at the longest fetch of open ocean on this planet, waters that only shearwaters, storm-petrels, and arctic terns know well.

In October of 2006, I jumped at the chance to spend a few days and nights on Mount Desert Rock, a stay extended a bit by bad weather. You cannot come and go as you please here. Those Zodiacs will take only so much bucking around in the swells. Getting on the Rock is a makeshift operation, at times a kind of controlled shipwreck. I went out with a ragtag group of birders and naturalists—good company—adventurous people who wanted to spend some time on what is, in effect, the farthest extension of the world of Mount Desert Island.

Those four days on Mount Desert Rock felt like the end of the beginning of my trying to appreciate and understand some things about this coast. Twenty-six miles offshore, I was pleased that I had gotten so far but was still in the same place. From a perch on the shelf rock, I could look out to sea, knowing there was nothing but water for thousands of miles. And I could turn around and take in the hand's-breadth of horizon that was Mount Desert. In the end, what's to say about such a place? It is enough that here on the coast of Maine, the sea comes to a conclusion, as does the land, each giving expert witness to the nature of things.

Spare as it was, Mount Desert Rock had extraordinary gifts to offer. Beyond some breaks for meals and conversation, there was nothing to do but watch the elements—land, water, sky. It's a fine if intimidating place to take the measure of yourself as an

observer, to see what you have inside yourself to meet this so
starkly drawn version of the world. There is nowhere to go on the
Rock except the Rock, and no distractions to protect you from
any emptiness in yourself or from any failure of your curiosity.
You had better be prepared to observe, to parse what you know
and do not know, and to let your thoughts and feelings get weathered in this extraordinary exposure.

I can only note a few things here, encounters on the Rock that
for me are at the outer margins of my experience of the world of
Mount Desert Island. There was the huge, red sun that rose from
the gulf one morning behind the *Katherine Louise*, a white lobster
boat with blue trim and an old-fashioned sternsail that I knew
it took some skill to use for holding a heading at a trap. There
was the sight of northern gannets plunge diving and the passage
of a northern fulmar, stockiest of the seabirds—a sturdy, Arctic
thing confident as a wolf. There was a *Mola mola*—a giant ocean
sunfish—that we saw from the lighthouse observation deck, a
tropical species that had wandered out of the Gulf Stream and was
caught in the inhospitable cold waters of the Gulf of Maine, where
it would die. One finback whale briefly surfaced into view at a
distance. Bluefin tuna eased by, feeding in graceful arcs through
a school of prey.

There were butterflies and bats and the gray seals and harbor
seals for which the Rock is home. There were varieties of sky I
have no language for, ways sunlight would play through clouds
and animate waves. There was the ominous, beautiful look of the
rising wind and seas that kept us on the island longer than we
planned to stay. We watched the seals get battered in that heavy
weather just offshore of the island and the next day saw their open

wounds when they were back up on the rocks. There was the tangible feel of hours passing somehow in all that expanse of moving stillness at the granite center of what felt like too much space, too much sky and water. When I got back to Mount Desert, I remember feeling claustrophobic for a day or two, and, driving to my cabin from Bar Harbor, the road seemed too narrow for my truck—a changed perception that felt nearly like a hallucination. And I remember that I didn't sleep well the first night back from the Rock because there was no foghorn trying to keep me awake.

There was more birdlife than I've ever seen in one place.* Ninety species came to or flew within view of this speck of land: seabirds, waterfowl, shorebirds, raptors, warblers, sparrows, wrens, doves, woodpeckers, blackbirds, birds of farm fields and deep woods, birds of eaves and alleyways. All found some temporary use for the Rock. Even if you were not interested in birds, you couldn't help but admire the intensity and variety of nature's avian imagination in a place where there was nothing else to do but watch and be instructed by the lives of things.

What are we looking for at the edge of the sea? Something in the world or something in us? Melville suggests that we are partly water and partly rock, partly fluid and partly static, that we are ourselves a beautiful, productive opposition like the land and the sea—a meeting place of contending, unfathomable energies. A fanciful thought, perhaps, or true.

The edge of the sea, particularly on these rocky coasts, is beautiful and harsh, like life. We evolved—by necessity and

---

* See the appendix for a complete list.

chance—at the edge of the sea in tidal zones stirred by the sun and the moon. Homesick, we come back to the sea, not just for the beauty but for the strangeness of it—the intimidating otherness of it—the uncanny way it takes us in and keeps us out. Every edge of Mount Desert Island—including the austere shore of Mount Desert Rock—is beautiful and strange in perfectly equal measure, like these gulls circling urgently in the moonlight, like these bruised seals keening under the stars.

Appendix

The Birds of Mount Desert Rock
October 3–6, 2006

Common loon
Razorbill
Black guillemot
Double-crested cormorant
Great cormorant

Canada goose
Green-winged teal
White-winged scoter
Surf scoter
Black scoter
Common eider
Red-breasted merganser

Greater shearwater
Sooty shearwater
Northern fulmar

Leach's storm-petrel
Northern gannet
Pomarine jaeger

Herring gull
Ring-billed gull
Black-legged kittiwake
Greater black-backed gull
Lesser black-backed gull

Common tern

Great blue heron

Ruddy turnstone
Semi-palmated plover
Greater yellowlegs
Sanderling
Pectoral sandpiper
Spotted sandpiper
Least sandpiper
White-rumped sandpiper

Sharp-shinned hawk
Northern harrier
Osprey
Kestrel
Merlin
Peregrine falcon

Mourning dove
Cuckoo (undetermined species)
Yellow-bellied sapsucker
Northern flicker

Eastern phoebe
Horned lark
American pipit
Tree swallow
Brown creeper
House wren
Winter wren
Carolina wren
Ruby-crowned kinglet
Golden-crowned kinglet
American robin
Catharus thrush (dark-backed Swainson type)
Hermit thrush
Brown thrasher
Gray catbird
Cedar waxwing
Red-eyed vireo
Blue-headed vireo

Blackpoll warbler
Black throated blue warbler
Yellow-rumped (myrtle) warbler
Cape May warbler
American redstart

Palm warbler
Orange-crowned warbler
Common yellowthroat
Yellow-breasted chat

American goldfinch
Purple finch

White-throated sparrow
Chipping sparrow
Field sparrow
Swamp sparrow
Clay-colored sparrow
Grasshopper sparrow
Song sparrow
Vesper sparrow
Lincoln's sparrow
Savannah sparrow

Dark-eyed junco
Lapland longspur
Rusty blackbird
Baltimore oriole
Dicksisel
Bobolink

This trip list was compiled by Lysle Brinker and is the composite of observations by Lysle Brinker, Chuck Whitney, Toby Stephenson, Bill Sheehan, Denny Abbott, Russell Mount, Chad Probst, John Fuller, and the author.

Sources

EPIGRAPH

Voyages of Samuel de Champlain 1604–1618, ed. W. L. Grant (New York: Charles Scribner's Sons, 1907), p. 45.

FIRST LIGHT

Elizabeth Bishop, *The Complete Poems 1927–1979* (New York: Farrar, Straus and Giroux, 1983), p. 3.

AT SHIP HARBOR

Robinson Jeffers, *Selected Poems* (New York: Random House/ Vintage, 1965), p. 4.

Samuel Eliot Morison, *The Story of Mount Desert Island* (French-boro, ME: Islandport Press, 2001), p. 103.

Selected Writings of Emerson, ed. Donald McQuade (New York: Modern Library, 1981), p. 390. The phrase is from "Nature," Essays: Second Series.

Rachel Carson, *The Edge of the Sea* (Boston: Houghton Mifflin, 1955), pp. 1, 2.

SUMMITS

Bishop, *The Complete Poems*, p. 93.

IRONBOUND COAST

Pathmakers: Cultural Landscape Report for the Historic Hiking Trail System of Mount Desert Island, prepared by Margaret Coffin Brown and the Olmsted Center for Landscape Preservation (Boston: National Park Service, 2006), p. 21.

James Dickey, "The Strength of Fields," *The Whole Motion: Collected Poems, 1945–1992* (Hanover, NH, and London: Wesleyan University Press/University Press of New England, 1992), p. 379.

SURFACINGS

Herman Melville, *Moby-Dick*, Norton Critical Edition, ed. Hershel Parker and Harrison Hayford (New York: W. W. Norton, 2002), pp. 218, 119.

The Complete Works of Captain John Smith (1580–1631) (3 vols.), ed. Philip L. Barbour, vol. I, (Chapel Hill: University of North Carolina Press, 1986), p. 323.

J. Hector St. John de Crèvecoeur, *Letters from an American Farmer* (Oxford and New York: Oxford University Press, 1997), p. 122.

Mark Kurlansky, *Cod: A Biography of the Fish That Changed the World* (New York: Penguin Books, 1998), p. 233.

MARSH TIME

Jim Harrison, *Saving Daylight* (Port Townsend, WA: Copper Canyon Press, 2006), p. 35.

RIVER OF MOUNTAINS

Bishop, *The Complete Poems*, p. 67.

PARALLAX

A. R. Ammons, *The Selected Poems: 1951–1977* (New York: W. W. Norton, 1977), p. 35.

LONG LEDGE

The Basic Works of Aristotle, ed. Richard McKeon (New York: Modern Library, 2001), p. 635.

DOWN EAST

Voyages of Samuel de Champlain, p. 29.

The Works of Samuel de Champlain (7 vols.), ed. H. P. Biggar et al., vol. I (Toronto: University of Toronto Press, 1971), pp. 241–43, 281.

The Voyage of Christopher Columbus: Columbus' Own Journal of Discovery, restored and translated by John Cummins (New York: St. Martin's Press, 1992), passim.

The Journal of John Winthrop, 1630–1649, ed. Richard S. Dunn, James Savage, and Laetitia Yeandle (Cambridge: The Belknap Press of Harvard University Press, 1996), p. 19.

John James Audubon: Writings and Drawings, Library of America edition (New York: Literary Classics of the United States, 1999), pp. 394, 396, 397.

CAIRNS

Moon in a Dewdrop: Writings of Zen Master Dōgen, ed. Kazuaki Tanahashi (New York: North Point Press/Farrar, Straus and Giroux, 1985), p. 107.

William Wordsworth, *Selected Poems and Prefaces*, ed. Jack Stillinger (Boston: Houghton Mifflin/Riverside, 1965), p. 109. The quotation is from "Tintern Abbey."

TOWARD *PEMETIC*

Charles G. Leland, *The Algonquin Legends of New England: Or, Myths and Folk Lore of the Micmac, Passamaquoddy, and Penobscot Tribes* (1884; repr., Charleston, SC: Bibliobazaar, 2006), pp. 34, 108, 115, 43, 66, 34, 57, 45.

2006 Waponahki Student Art Show: A Collaboration of Maine Indian Education and the Abbe Museum (Bar Harbor, ME: Maine Indian Education/Abbe Museum, 2006). Kelsey Anne Shepard is quoted on p. 6.

LAST LIGHT

Melville, *Moby-Dick*, p. 225.

Journal of John Winthrop, p. 32.

Charles B. McLane, *Islands of the Mid-Maine Coast, Volume II: Mount Desert to Machias Bay* (Falmouth, ME: Kennebec River Press, 1989), p. 101.

Other Reading

For a more detailed account of indigenous prehistory and coastal history, I highly recommend Bruce J. Bourque, *Twelve Thousand Years: American Indians in Maine* (Lincoln and London: University of Nebraska Press, 2001); Frank G. Speck, *Penobscot Man* (Orono: University of Maine Press, 1998); Roger F. Duncan, *Coastal Maine: A Maritime History* (Woodstock, VT: Countryman Press, 2002). George B. Dorr's *The Story of Acadia National Park* (Bar Harbor, ME: Acadia Publishing, 1997) is a brief memoir of his pioneering efforts to create a national park on Mount Desert Island. Russell Butcher's *Field Guide to Acadia National Park, Maine,* revised edition (Lanham, MD: Taylor Trade Publishing, 2005), is an excellent introduction to the natural history of the park. Les Watling, Jill Fegley, and John Moring's *Life Between the Tides: Marine Plants and Animals of the Northeast* (Gardiner, ME: Tilbury House, 2003) and Loren C. Petry and Marcia G. Norman's *A Beachcomber's Botany* (Chatham, MA: Chatham Conservation Foundation, 1968) are very useful for parsing the life of the shore. Although it hasn't been updated in more than twenty years, Ralph H. Long's *Native Birds of Mount Desert Island and Acadia National Park* (Mount Desert, ME: Ralph H. Long,

1987) is still a wonderful companion to any birding on the island. Weekly nature columns by Ruth Grierson and Scott Grierson, which appear in the *Mount Desert Islander* and the *Bar Harbor Times*, respectively, have for years provided residents and visitors with lively accounts of Mount Desert's flora and fauna. Marilyn J. Dwelley's *Trees and Shrubs of New England* (Camden, ME: Down East Books, 2000) is very useful. For insight and information on the islands of the coast of Maine, see Charles McLane's *Islands of the Mid-Maine Coast, Volume II: Mount Desert to Machias Bay* (Falmouth, ME: Kennebec River Press, 1989) and Philip W. Conkling's *Islands in Time: A Natural and Cultural History of the Islands of the Gulf of Maine*, revised edition (Camden, ME: Down East Books, 1999). A recent account of the natural history and current plight of the Gulf of Maine can be found in David Dobbs, *The Great Gulf: Fishermen, Scientists, and the Struggle to Revive the World's Greatest Fishery* (Washington, DC: Island Press/Shearwater Books, 2000). Beyond the standard field guides, Peter Harrison's *Seabirds: An Identification Guide*, revised edition (Boston: Houghton Mifflin, 1985), is indispensable for getting into pelagic bird-watching. For pursuing an interest in marine mammals in the Mount Desert area there is Steven Katona, Valerie Rough, and David Richardson's excellent *A Field Guide to Whales, Porpoises, and Seals from Cape Cod to Newfoundland*, fourth edition, revised (Washington and London: Smithsonian Institution Press, 1993). Jennifer Alisa Paigen's *The Sea Kayaker's Guide to Mount Desert Island* (Camden, ME: Down East Books, 1997) is indispensable for getting started as an offshore paddler in these wonderful waters. Dolores Kong and Dan Ring's *Hiking Acadia National Park* (Guilford, CT: Globe Pequot Press, 2001) will get you to the terrestrial trailheads. Pamela Belanger's *Inventing Acadia: Artists and Tourists at Mount Desert* (Rockland, ME: Farnsworth Art Museum, 1999) is a superb history of the island, with many fine illustrations of the art it has inspired, including Thomas Doughty's paintings of Mount Desert Rock.

Franklin Pierce University

00203081